Diana Crighton's

English Excursions

which inspire and refresh

D0522633

Home Counties
& London

Excursion | Publishing

Acknowledgements

I would like to thank all my friends who have encouraged and supported the idea of this book, particularly José Northey, Liz Randall and Geoff Hyde. Without the generous help of the owners, directors, keepers, curators and managers of the places which I am privileged to visit, and who responded readily to all my questions, this would have been a different book. I am very grateful to Cassandra Kent for her encouragement and editing, Mitou Tricoit for her exceedingly hard work and imagination with the design, John Montgomery for his delightful illustrations and Leonard Chave for his scrutiny. I thank Howard Martin, Principal Lecturer in History of Architecture at Kingston University for reading the manuscript and his suggestions and Allan Powers. I appreciate the help given by Joan Harding and Anne Grace of Domestic Buildings Research Group. Not least I wish to record the kindness of all those I stay with when travelling and the help given by my long suffering local librarians.

Illustration John Montgomery
Design Mitou Tricoit
Printing Leicester Printers Ltd

©1996 Diana Crighton
First Published in Great Britain 1996

Excursion Publishing
PO Box 351, Richmond, Surrey TW10 7YY

ISBN 0-9528334-0-9

Contents

Signpost to Excursions

I was quite young when bitten by the excursion bug. On Fridays after school we were taken to our local museums. One had a marvellous portico, yet terrifying *'mummies'*. However, in those days few cultural places had tea-rooms so we feasted at tea-shops or smart stores on sticky iced-lemon buns, toasted buttered pikelets, meringues and cream horns. And the subsequent memories of *'bus walks'* from school in Sussex to Devil's Dyke, Elizabethan houses and castles or Empire Day picnics in char-à-bancs to Roman villas with our sandwiches in redundant gas-mask boxes, have also endured.

I have written for those who love diversity and colour, celebrating English style, traditions and taste in art and customs. I wanted to share some special places and the people who make each journey distinct, especially where there is synergy or connection between the place and the tea-rooms. I looked for an English all-through feeling, particularly in the country, food for the mind, eye and body.

Although tea-rooms at museums and historic sites encourage another form of eating they also have the opportunity to provide essential England; they can be endearing and seductive when they serve good food. I hunt out character, customs, quality and quirks. Visiting can also be a lark! I prefer honest unpretentious victuals, not phoney glamour or the place so aptly expressed by Ogden Nash where:

'There's the parsley cluttering up your food
and the problem is to get it off without being rude.'

Fortunately visiting special places is a large part of my work and what I look for are a sense of place, a pervading spirit and a heartfelt welcome. As for food, good tea, real coffee not *'puddle water'*, muscular cheese and fuelling bread are imperative. A homemade dish is best, soup will do and two or three scrunchy salads. Who would not choose clotted cream rather than the spray-gun variety, the intense flavour of homemade raspberry jam with fresh scones and a bounty of butter? Not standardised, not uniform, not processed but fresh and regional. I look for must-have homemade cakes, seasonal dishes, the indigenous traditions and merits of English cooking. Who craves imported apples whilst English orchards still survive? Let us help their survival. In England we have year-round vegetables with enviable flavour. Ambrose Heath suggested that May was the gastronomic start of the *'Annus Edibilis';* I propose that the subsequent fruits of June and bliss of July's fruit and vegetables are positively promoted in the tea-rooms. Each food like each place has its finest moment. Good value and a caring attitude are just as vital and as the days of hibernation are over, more locations, even gardens, could open for visitors during the closed season.

We shall visit places which reflect England's character, a tapestry of landscape, buildings and food influenced by climate and topography woven with threads of other cultures. This is an engrossing and connecting theme. The will and determination of the conquering Normans not only shaped the country with castles and cathedrals but also influenced our language and diet. Inigo Jones, who visited Italy, was the catalyst for the classical renaissance, English Palladian, seen in several of the houses we visit. Whilst the magnificent legacy of the 18th century houses, built by noblemen to parade their position, were also frequently the result of travel, foreign trade or the Grand Tour. When I read about a culinary connection with The Duke of Newcastle, prime minister to George II, Claremont and Paris, 18th century manners and taste came alive.

I am indebted to many writers and diarists: John Evelyn and Samuel Pepys, Parson Woodforde, Horace Walpole, William

Cobbett, and of course Jane Austen who with their observations and wit furnished some intriguing connections. All buildings, however, reflect social history and change just as the food and customs at another stratum of society late in the 19th century recorded by Flora Thompson in Oxfordshire and Reverend John Coker Egerton in Sussex are, I consider, equally appealing.

I hope this will please the country-minded and city-rooted. I hope it encourages lingering, return journeys and a quest for quality and that in making this choice I have included idiosyncrasies and ingredients that you will want to experience. This book is for the curious, those who like clues, rather than those who want everything on a plate.

Future volumes of English Excursions will feature the Northern, Midland and South Western counties where much of my work has taken me over the last few years. I am itching to write about the exquisite Geffrye Museum, the only one in England showing middle class furniture and decorative arts in a sequence of period rooms, which is building an extension that will include a new restaurant. With all the exciting developments in London there will surely be even more complete excursions.

In memory of my father who loved England.

Bath

Berkshire

Gloucestershire

Hampshire

Oxfordshire

Roman Baths Museum and Pump Room

Bath

What pleasure to make the decision *'to Bath'* at breakfast and by mid-morning to be able to take coffee in the Pump Room accompanied by a trio playing suitable salon music. Bath is the appropriate curtain raiser to this book. *'Travellers come to see it for it is beyond compare'*, wrote Arthur Mee. No other city has achieved this fame in England. Bath is the symbiosis of many themes in this book — food, literature, architecture, new influences, travel-manners and all. Here we first meet some of the key players, illustrious figures, intellectuals, writers, scientists of the 18th century age of reason and enlightenment. Politicians, actors, artists, inventors lived, passed through and socialised in Bath. They include William Wilberforce, William Oliver, a fellow of the Royal Society and Sir William Herschel who discovered the planet Uranus from his garden in 1781, Jane Austen, Thomas Gainsborough, Lord Clive the explorer and General Wolfe of Quebec. Bath is a historic monument conceived principally by John Wood elder and younger, a Georgian destination laid out without want of funds, the place to reside, continuing to attract writers through the 19th century and today.

The only hot springs in England may have been discovered 800 years before the Romans discovered Aqua Sulis. In AD54 they constructed these magnificent buildings, temple and great hall. The pavements surrounding the baths and culverts are still in use as originally designed to take unused water back to the Avon. In the 12th century their use was recorded by Henry of Huntington, not just for the infirm who gathered to take the waters that were beneficial but *'persons in health also assemble there, to see the curious bubbling up of the warm springs and to use the Baths'*. The exciting treasures that came to light in 1882 — the Roman sculpture, ceramics and jewels — are very well presented in the Museum. One of the first discoveries was a bronze head of Minerva unearthed in

1727 which would have been sited in the temple, now the site of the Pump Room. Just over 100 years ago the baths were re-discovered lying 15 feet below the city. Indeed when Jane Austen and her contemporaries assembled in Bath the Roman Baths were not known.

The Georgian new swept the medieval past away, there are few narrow lanes in Bath. However, just beside the Pump Room is the beautiful Bath Abbey with west front and principally decorated 15th century style on the site of an earlier Norman cathedral built in 1090, some four years before Winchester. It is admired for its wonderful 52 windows and early fan-vaulting in the chancel and transepts. Later in the 19th century the Abbey was restored by Sir Giles Gilbert Scott.

Bath was the pinnacle of 18th century taste and design, principally through the work and promotion of the architects John Wood, Beau Nash, man of fashion, lawyer and benefactor and Ralph Allen, patron entrepreneur who made his fortune from Bath stone and carrying mail via the mail coach. Taking the waters was already popular for curative purposes but now it became *'a sport and a diversion'*. Music played whilst visitors took the water in the King's Bath, *'stripped to the smock'* at the fashionable hours between 8 and 10am. The success of Bath reflected a plentiful land, peace, inventions and innovations. It was the first example of complete town planning, a homogeneous town of golden ashlar stone. The first English squares by the two John Woods were described by Nikolaus Pevsner as *'the first after Inigo Jones to impose Palladian uniformity on an English Square as whole'*. These influences are celebrated firstly in Queen Square in 1728 and later The Circus and Royal Crescent. Looking at the last you will see the *'palace front'*, a seamless façade as though one building, designed by John Wood the younger, which also related importantly with the landscape, sloping lawns in front providing a contrast to the closed squares. As a French traveller put it in 1810 *'the town looks as though it has been cast in a mould all at once ... where most of the inhabitants appeared to do nothing except frequent the splendid shops and kill time'*. At the end of the streets, vistas take the eye to parks and wooded hills. Nature was nearby and encompassed in Georgian Bath which still has many parks and gardens. The Sydney Gardens rivalled Ranelagh and Vauxhall Gardens in London for their profit-making events. Tickets were sold in advance for public breakfasts. At Bath we first meet Robert Adam who refurbished Osterley (see page 45). His Pulteney bridge with shops built across both sides is a rare example of an Italian concept in England and more of his designs can be seen at the Guildhall in the interior of the Banqueting Hall.

The civility and gentility of the Pump Room designed by John Palmer and Thomas Baldwin was the epitomy of 18th century fashion and taste, now happily a far cry from James Lees Milne's description just after the war: *'dirty, dingy and neglected'*. His later plea that there *'should be gay music and inviting coffee and biscuits'* has come right. This and the Assembly Rooms which now contain the Museum of Costume were the hub of structured society, being the places to parade, to dally, to make acquaintances and pursue pleasure. In Jane Austen's *Northanger Abbey* the purpose was confirmed: *'to make enquiries and to receive intelligence, where gentlemen talked over the politics of the day and compared accounts of their newspapers whilst ladies walked about together, noticing every new face and almost every new bonnet'*.

Today papers are set out for visitors, the trio plays, not intrusively, rather to enhance the mood of the company, but there is an insufficiency of hats! However, charming waitresses rapidly replace the white tablecloths, bring you pots of coffee and Bath buns, hot chocolate and cinnamon biscuits. If you are encouraged to linger and eat lunch in winter, steak and kidney pudding, treacle pudding and many dishes with a continental slant are prepared. One wonders how Jane Austen would have reacted, as she has a wry comment about French bread in *Northanger Abbey*. Bath spa water, Bath sausages and homemade Bath biscuits are served with English and foreign cheeses. It is civilising to sit in the elegant carpeted room with the buzz of conversation on Chippendale seats surrounded by portraits. The waters are now served by the pumper employed by the caterers. This was formerly a civic post. With the Tompian clock and Corinthian pilasters, it is easy to imagine the parade and entertainment of the 18th century.

Bath has a goodly selection of Museums and a wonderful Victorian Art Gallery with a collection of works by British painters, Victorian genre and a small but beautiful collection of glass. Nearby in Milsom Street is the Royal Photographic Society's Octagon Galleries which keep an important collection of 19th century work both English and French. The works of the pictorialist George Martin, Cartes de Visite, a fashion of the 1850s, by André Adolphe-Eugène Disdéri, *'Flowers and Fruit'* by Roger Fenton, early cameras and examples of W. H. Fox Talbot's calotypes. This collection and exhibitions are presented on two levels of the Octagon Gallery which was formerly a chapel.

The new café is an aesthetic contrast to the Pump Room, furnished with Jacobsen-influenced chairs, hung with photographs by Julia Margaret Cameron, including one of G. F. Watts and a constant rolling small screen of the collection's immortals — Parkinson, Beaton and Cameron. I am not convinced about the all-day jazz — tapes not live — perhaps this will abate or there will be breaks for auditory comfort. Obviously a good meeting place for members, intimate with good food. One or two light dishes, toasted muffins, more Bath sausages and Bath cheese, decent salads with recognisable crisp ingredients as well as a mushroom risotto are fitting. The freshly squeezed juices of red pepper, tomato and carrot or a blend of melons are welcome for the atmosphere is warm.

Bath is still seriously diverting, continues its tradition and keeps its eyes and ears open for what is happening in the world of taste and style.

The Roman Baths and Pump Room

Stall Street Bath BA1 1LX. Tel 01225 477785 Fax 01225 444793.
Baths and Pump Room open: April-Sept 9-6. Aug late evening opening 8-10.
Oct-Mar 10-5, Sun 10.30-5.
Admission charge to Baths.
The Pump Room: seats 120. Free admission.
Rail: Bath Spa.
Bus: Bath Bus station.
Road: A4

The Royal Photographic Society, Octagon Galleries

Milsom Street, Bath BSA1 1DN. Tel 01225 462841 Fax 01225 448688.
Open: daily from 9.30-5.30 except 25-26 Dec. Last admission 4.45.
Admission charge to Galleries.
Café: seats 55. Open: 9.30-5.

The American Museum in Britain

Bath

This museum, housed in the Manor, sits high on the Downs, overlooking the Avon Valley. Claverton Manor is a beautiful Neo-Classical house designed in 1820 by Sir Jeffrey Wyattville, with parkland and a wooded estate of 122 acres. He built many houses in the Gothic style and even incorporated sham fortifications into Windsor Castle. However, his client at Claverton, John Vivian, must have wanted the Classical style. Wyattville persuaded him to pull down the former Jacobean Manor, in a state of disrepair, and build anew in a healthier and more picturesque situation where the aspect was all. But Vivian's son George, a connoisseur who took the Grand Tour was opposed to the plan and contrived to have several pictures of the old Manor painted before its destruction. One, fortunately in the Museum's keeping, can still be seen. The Bath stone mansion and the setting are a delight and the gardens are inspirational. One is an exact replica of George Washington's Mount Vernon, with a heady perfume of roses, clove pinks and lavender in summer.

The Museum opened in 1961. Its objective was to interpret both the social and art history of the United States. It has a blissful collection of American quilts, historical maps, exquisitely furnished rooms and a research library. I find the journey through 16 settings, each telling a different story of social history through decorative arts a great pleasure. A Greek revival room shows examples by Duncan Phyfe of American Neo-Classic style furniture; the late 18th century parlour has an elegant secretary and contemporary sampler. There is a Shaker room, where the simplicity of the furniture has inspired some of today's furniture designers; a chair hangs on the wall. The New Mexican Room shows how a colonist's house would have looked, with an example of a chest designed to store all household effects. Another room, the tavern, has a commodious dresser and a beehive oven still used to bake George Washington's mother's gingerbread recipe. All this and the 17th century Keeping Room, which was the family living and dining room of the Puritan founding fathers, make this visit distinctive.

I always have one potent visual memory of each place that I visit. At Claverton I recall the quilts, a vast collection, which are well presented for easy viewing. In a ground floor wing there is a gallery of folk art such as decoy ducks, and railway and pub signs, showing another aspect of American decorative art. The rooms are not large, more like visual vignettes of each period, and therefore make an attractive excursion for children. This is not a place to rush through. I am a devotee and have visited several times, but still find it hard to leave. Everyone who works here appears to love it.

The cooking in the country kitchen is just as it should be — real. A wooden hand-painted board lists the goodies. There are no packets of pre-mixed cakes, or ready-baked and reheated catering items; these are entirely evocative, home-baked aromas, not bottled. I cannot resist the smell of chocolate brownies, Hurry

Up gingerbread, George Washington cake or a spicy fruit cake entitled a *great cake*; the recipe book is for sale so you can practise at home. The staff serve from rather a modest counter and through a large window in the serving area you can look into the kitchen and see them preparing food at a large wooden table. We tend to forget the importance of large tables for baking. No high tech here, at least not yet! And there is no food of the other American variety, which has taken over English high streets. American visitors tell me

they are surprised to see the scale of this invasion into our sub-
urbs and on every corner of small towns, a scale larger than on
the other side of the Atlantic. At Bath you will find American
country cooking of the cookie and tea bread variety. Try several
if you are in a party: corn bread, Georgia nut bread and orange
butter cookies. Above all this is an authoritative cultural connection as the food really does reflect the history behind the exhibits.

I prefer to sit and take lunch or tea on the terrace, overlooking the marvellous downs. The service is accomplished and
friendly. Most of the staff have been here a long time and their
loyalty to the Museum is evident.

The American Museum in Britain

Claverton Manor, Bath BA2 7BD. Tel 01225 460503 Fax 01225 480726.
Open: March to early Nov 2-5 daily except Mon.
Admission charge to Museum. Reduced fee for grounds, Folk Art, New Gallery and
tea-room.
Tea-room: seats 60 inside, 40 terrace. Open 2-5.
Nearest railway station: Bath.
Bus: 18.
Road: A46. Parking: 400 yards.

Basildon Park

Berkshire

Successful merchants have built their houses hereabouts for 200 years, along the upper reaches of the Thames. First, Sir Francis Sykes of the East India Company built at Basildon between 1776 and 1783. Later the Victorian merchants built their solid and reassuring half-timbered medieval-revival brick family houses in the 1890s. Seven of these along the stretch at Pangbourne are now known locally as the *'seven deadly sins'* and the best way to see them is from a boat on the river. History has come full circle; East has travelled West and today vice versa as many of the large houses in the area are now owned by Middle Eastern businessmen.

The long wooded drive up to Basildon Park does not provide all the clues to the delights of this perfect Palladian house, in mellowing Bath stone. This was designed by John Carr of York and is a rare example of his work in the South of England. On a sunny day, it is one of his best, most inspiring and original façades, to be seen and cherished. It is a sight for city eyes. The house is formed with a central block, and has a double-height portico which sits above a rusticated loggia. The side wings, or pavilions, are linked via a single-story curtain wall, behind which are two small courtyards; one is used as a tea-terrace in the summer. Basildon looks beautiful in its setting and is a tribute to Francis Sykes who chose such a fortunate position which looks over the valley, lawns and woodland, with willow and ilex bordering the river Thames.

This house has an interesting history, a mixture of lavish care and neglect reflecting the changing fortunes of its owners. Sir Francis Sykes' grandson not only lost the family fortune, he may also have inspired a literary character. There are rumours that his profligacy, conduct and treatment of his wife provided a model for the despicable Bill Sykes in Charles Dickens' *Oliver Twist*.

In the 19th century a string of architects made successive changes after James Morrison bought the house in 1838. He had built a very successful wholesale haberdashery in a short space of time having fortuitously married Mary Anne Todd, his employer's daughter. Morrison met J. B. Papworth, the architect whom he appointed to complete Carr's design when Papworth had been a young employee designing handkerchiefs at Todd & Co. Morrison himself started here as a shop man. Morrison was not only a shrewd businessman but also cultivated in the arts and numbered John Stuart Mill and J. M. W. Turner, who stayed at Basildon, among his friends. He became a respected figure and bridged the divide between arts and manufacturing and served among others on the first School of Industrial Design at Somerset House, the forerunner of the Victoria and Albert museum. Morrison had several houses but wanted another nearer London and Basildon became an alternative town house, served by the new railway from London to Bristol.

Morrison purchased the works of Lorrain, Rubens and Rembrandt but did not seemingly entertain lavishly. (A Constable that he bought for 150 guineas was recently sold for 9.5 million.) He kept only six or seven servants, even less than some of his tenants, whilst Parson Woodforde kept five in his modest household. Thomas Coke of Holkham, however, employed at least 60 in 1820. Perhaps Morrison preferred small parties and debate rather than entertaining on a grand scale.

During the Second World War country houses were used to store national art collections, troops and schools. Basildon itself housed soldiers and even prisoners of war and then became derelict. Fortunately it continued to attract owners who cared deeply about the house and its decoration. After the War it was bought by Lord and Lady Iliffe, lovingly refurbished, and was given to the National Trust in 1987. The Iliffes took great care to collect doors from other Carr houses, which fitted perfectly, they bought textiles from sale rooms and incorporated their own collections. The total look of interior furnishing is quite appropriate and a feast for the eyes.

The most striking features are the Great Staircase and Hall

where the importance of arrival and of entering the house are emphasised. As guests ascended the double flight of stairs, from the loggia, they saw the ornate plasterwork of the gallery above them. There are other beautifully furnished rooms: the Octagon Drawing Room, where three projecting large windows give splendid views of the Thames, has a gilded frieze by Papworth. In the dining room a beautiful scagliola inlay — pink and white — above the chimney piece can be seen in the room which was used only on grand occasions, with a collection of some of Sir Francis Sykes' Chinese Export ware. Today these rooms are perfumed with fresh flowers.

The personal welcome received at arrival continues in the tea-room, situated in the lower hall next to the former servants' quarters where the dining area gives you a view onto parkland. (The original kitchen, located in the North Pavilion, was too far for practical use in the 20th century.) Those who have seen The Victorian Kitchen Garden series on television will remember Ruth Mott, who cooked in this house. I like to imagine that her pragmatic approach and respect for good ingredients have left a legacy here. They use some of her recipes. Homely food is the order of the day, served informally and popular with locals (always a good sign). Hot food, soup and generous portions of deep flans and salad are served at lunch. The texture and taste of soup with chunks of carrot and onion recalls the soups mothers used to make, and some still do, before *'Cup of Soup'*! The food counter area is utilitarian, of the Formica era, but this does not cause a problem because the cakes which are displayed here and the smell of baking are enticing. The space, with its original floor and solid furniture, although pleasing, could be brighter, and needs more heat in autumn. However, the atmosphere is friendly and the staff are keen to please. For those who are also fascinated about the owners of this house, a local historian has written a *History of Basildon*, an archive containing pictorial and written evidence on the estate which visitors can see by making an appointment.

Basildon Park

Lower Basildon, Reading, Berkshire RG8 9NR. Tel 01734 843040 Fax 01734 841267.
Open: end March-end Oct: Wed-Sat 2-6, Sun & BH Mon 12-6.
Admission charge. Free to NT members.
Tea-room: seats 80. Open: Wed-Fri 2-5.30, Sun & BH Mon 12-5.30.
Exhibition: Mon & Tues afternoon by appointment.
Rail: Pangbourne.
Bus: 105 Reading - Pangbourne.
Road: M4 J12. Parking 400 yards. Disabled parking nr house.

Arlington Mill Museum

Gloucestershire

Bibury is the quintessential English village. Almost 100 years ago it was popularised in *A Cotswold Village*, written by Arthur Gibbs in 1898. It deserves its place on the list of the most beautiful places in England. The village has all the right ingredients: the idyllic, almost out of a watercolour but real Arlington Row, which faces the River Coln; the Mill, built in the 17th century originally for fulling cloth and later for grinding corn; a wonderful scene of Cotswold stone, which H. J. Massingham described as *'the tone-rhythm for all Cotswold life'*; a Norman church with Saxon origins, the Swan Hotel's delightful gardens, the sound of water and several hostelries.

William Morris, who lived nearby at Kelmscott, described Bibury as *'the prettiest Village in England'*. Bibury invites everyone to stand and stare, and take refreshment of the culinary kind. It captivates even more on a late summer evening, when the hordes have gone home. Arlington Row was built in the 14th century as one long sheep house and was later occupied by weavers. It is now a row of cottages in the care of The National Trust and appears to grow out of the meadow, Rack Isle, where the woven cloth was hung out on racks to dry, opposite the bridge.

The Mill is a privately-run social history museum, with an interesting collection of photographs, millstones, pulleys, its own ghost and a tea-room. It is situated just near the bridge, next to the trout farm. A climb up the stairs of the Mill, through the exhibits, brings you out to a tea-terrace which looks over the mill wheel. The environment and sound of water will refresh anyone who has toiled on a hot motorway.

The tea-room is modest; one or two cakes are displayed on a trolley, made locally, plus trout paté from the farm and local ice-cream. There are cream teas, and ham or smoked fillets of trout with salad. In winter, tea is served on the ground floor, which looks out on to the mill wheel, so creaking timbers replace the sound of gushing water in this season. The trout hatcheries next door are over 90 years old. Their founder Arthur Severn, a cousin of John Ruskin, combined this business with the Mill.

Competition is tough for those who ply the hospitality trade, and service *has* to be friendly. Because the tea-room is small, it is worth booking ahead if you have a party, as Bibury is busy in high summer and parking is difficult. The best view of the whole village is from the Burford side of Bibury where an hour or so spent looking at the buildings, watching the trout, taking lunch or tea, is inspirational and refreshing. The Cotswold stone still shines on a sunny January day, though with a softer hue, and Bibury makes a good winter excursion as the Mill opens when most comparable places nearby have battened down their hatches.

At the other end of the village is Bibury Court, built in 1633 for Sir Thomas Sackville and now an hotel with elegant grounds. The church next door dates from the 11th century. It moved Alec Clifton-Taylor, one of the most inspiring architectural historians, to write that *'the churchyard was perhaps the most enchanting in England'*. It is far better to see this village on foot. Bibury is well placed between Burford, another favourite of mine, and Cirencester where there is a superb cheese stall at the Monday market as well as the famous, ornate triple-decker wool church porch and more attractive buildings in this inspiring stone.

Arlington Mill Museum

Bibury, nr Cirencester, Gloucestershire GL7 5NL. Tel 01285 740368.
Opens: daily 10-6.
Admission charge.
Tea-room: seats 60. Open: 10-5.30.
Road: A40. Parking limited in village.

Ruskin Mill

Gloucestershire

Squeezed in between one of the old steep packhorse roads and the river Frome facing upstream, just off the road approaching Nailsworth, is this charming early 19th century mill. It now serves a different purpose as a base and centre for arts, crafts and environmental development. The sound of running water masks the noise of the traffic and the conjunction of building, water and wooded valley inspires the artists and craftspeople who work here. Leather work, stained glass and sculpture are displayed for anyone to see in changing exhibitions. As the name suggests, the teachings of John Ruskin and also William Morris are fundamental to Ruskin Mill. Morris' question *'What business have we with art at all unless all can share it?'* and his dictum that the craftsman maker should experience as much happiness as the user, applies at the Mill. Ruskin, like Morris, was opposed to the effect of the machine on handicrafts. He provides a connection with the ethics of the Mill and Oxford University to which he gave several of his pictures by Turner. For nine years he was Slade Professor of Art at Oxford where he founded the Ruskin School of Drawing.

On one sunny morning I found an unusual blend of landscape and food. Organic vegetables and virtually organic-reared trout are sold and the philosophy is to respect all the good things that grow. This is a perfect place to gain refreshment, away from fret and bustle both visually and physically. You can eat here, buy bread and vegetables, look over the water and reedbeds and book a guided tour of the watermill. Ruskin Mill is one of those places where you can sit and let the day stretch out endlessly before you.

Nailsworth, a former Cotswold woollen town, is a pleasant place from which you can walk and enjoy the delights of Minchinhampton Common and village. The Mill has a bright little coffee shop at the top of a flight of stairs, with wooden furniture and a deck-like terrace, giving a wonderful view over the river. The food is fresh every day and changes according to the seasons and who is cooking. I like this approach. Most of the ingredients are organic and the staff work in a small kitchen behind the counter and are prepared to talk about food. On one visit they were making fresh basil and tomato soup, large flans and there was a tempting smell of baking. The end result includes thick date slices, chocolate and fruit cakes. Certainly this is the place to fill your basket with goodies from the organic produce shop, free-range eggs, fruit and vegetables.

The importance of good nutrition, good ingredients and their effect on the quality of life will permeate anyone who stops here. They aim to educate and help young people with problems by underlining the importance of good food. The students work in the food and coffee shop as part of a learning process for those who do not have the opportunity at home to learn these funda-mental skills, which are being eroded by changes in society and ready-made foods. The organisers believe this ethos can help everyone to get back in touch with the joys of growing, cooking, handling and eating good food, especially through cooking, one of the most gratifying occupations for anyone.

Whilst in this mood you can travel further to stay at one of the best, among the countless, bed and breakfast establishments that I have stayed in. Gilberts, just north of Stroud is a late medieval house that was sympathetically restored with a real understanding of wood, in the idiom of the Arts and Crafts, by local carpenters, for the present owner's parents. The house is a great pleasure with its beautiful wood floors, doors, sitting room and stone fireplace, but the food is another matter. Jenny Beer keeps sheep in her orchard, chickens, bees (not fed sugar), and has a splendid fruit and vegetable garden, which feeds the guests. From this garden, throughout summer, ruby red fruits grace the table, plums, loganberries, blackcurrants with bowls of yoghurt, warm wholemeal rolls, and compotes of the fruit in winter, with honey from the hives. As Jenny writes on the breakfast menu *'mushroom from the fields when the fairies favour'*, nor does *'the breakfast come off the peg'*. The genuinely delicious organic breakfast includes sausages, eggs, Gilberts' own tomatoes and farm-pressed apple juice, which you can buy with a Gilberts' pot of honey.

Whenever I stay I am allowed to unwind with a pot of tea before I unpack. Outside the peace is slightly marred if I sit topping and tailing fruit on the step, by the hum of the M5. However, all rooms are double glazed, and guests can sit at the scrubbed kitchen table with its Aga and in the sitting room. This is no modern put-u-up, just extraordinary refreshment. These words by Harold Munro could have been written for Gilberts:

> *'Your homely floor is creaking for our tread*
> *The smiling teapot with contented spout*
> *Thinks of boiling water, and the bread longs for butter ...'*

Ruskin Mill

Old Bristol Road, Nailsworth, Gloucestershire GL6 0LA. Tel 01453 832571
Fax 01453 835029.
No admission charge.
Open: daily 9-5.
Coffee-shop: seats 16 plus terrace. Open: daily (except Mon) 11-4, Sun 3-6.
Rail: Stroud.
Road: A46. Parking: outside.

Gilberts

Brookthorpe, nr Gloucester, Gloucestershire GL4 0UH. Tel & Fax 01452 812364.
Rail: Gloucester or Stroud.
Road: A4173.
Bus: from Gloucester or Stroud. Stop at end of lane.

Winchester Cathedral

Hampshire

H.V. Morton, describing Winchester in *In Search of England* wrote, *'if one were looking for the germ of the British Empire, it is to be found in this quiet little city of Winchester'*. He was probably right. No Empire today, nor little, but every visitor will feel the sense of stability that emanates from the history and intactness of a city within its walls. Not so quiet today, either, if you veer towards the commercial High Street but there are many peaceful lanes and small streets to be explored. Winchester was the premier city where English kings were crowned, before Westminster Hall and Abbey were built. Its architect bishop, William of Wykeham, was indirectly accountable for the hundreds of buildings forming Winchester College which he founded. This became the model for the English public school system whose buildings largely make up the unaltered picture we see today.

The character of the city grows from the College buildings, medieval, Tudor and Georgian, the city walls, ecclesiastical buildings and, most important, the Cathedral providing a rare architectural tapestry. In the arch of one of the two remaining city gates, King's Gate, there is one of the smallest churches I have ever seen — St Swithun's. The legend goes that if it rains on St Swithun's Day, July 15th, it will rain for 40 days, conversely if it shines, so the next 40 days will be fine! There are guided tours of some of the College buildings, including the Hall and chapel. I feel privileged to have worked with the College architect on some modifications to the original serving areas adjoining the Hall, so-called hatches that Bishop Wykeham built 600 years ago in 1396! I looked forward to every visit. Walks through meadows and streets lined with College buildings lead into the cobbled Cathedral Close where clergy, Dean and Chapter reside. The Close is a splendid combination of 17th, 18th and earlier houses; doorways in some of the walls afford glimpses of graceful gardens.

Winchester's magnificent Norman cathedral probably out-classes any other cathedral in England; the Norman part was completed in 1094, on St Swithun's Day. Daunting to think that only 14 years after William the Conqueror had landed at Pevensey, this cathedral was constructed. The memorable image is the Norman transept. The remains of some of the chapels and the crypt are also Norman. In the 14th century Bishop Wykeham completed the glorious west front and built the nave aisles.

A small door at the West End leads to some new and refurbished buildings. The modern refectory is built in glass with exposed steel beams and situated in a walled garden. Although the furniture is somewhat out of character, this is a brave piece of modern design and the locals approve. The food is well cooked, uses some local ingredients and is good value. The service is manned by a large army of volunteers. There are two counters; the light snack help yourself counter can be tricky for older visitors. However, staff serve the robust hot dishes and vegetables from the other counter which I believe is better value offering the kind of stalwart food you need for a city walk, as much as one in the country. Large open toasted sandwiches, called 'trenchers' are descendants of the medieval tranchoir where a thick piece of bread acts as a *'plate'*, on which a good helping of beef and horseradish, or pork sausages and potato salad, is piled. (Wooden trenchers are still used by the scholars at Winchester). I award plus points for the Hampshire ice-cream and child's portions, as well as homemade pizza and burgers, 'to keep them happy'.

Hampshire foods and customs rely heavily on the clear sparkling rivers, which still supply trout and watercress. The Romans planted vines and good strong ale is brewed. One family brewery remains. The gilded weathervane above the West

Gate, in the form of a pig, illustrates the Hampshire Hog's importance in this county. The diarist William Cobbett described the delights of fresh food when he reached Kings Worthy on 9th November 1825 where he saw a beautiful strawberry garden 'watered' by the nearby Itchen which he supposed had been diverted for this purpose. *Just by, on the greensward, is an alcove under very fine trees wherein to sit and eat strawberries coming from the little garden just mentioned, met by bowls of cream from a little milk house ... . What delight! What a terrestrial paradise!'*, terrestrial paradise indeed!

The Cathedral's ministry of welcome is complemented in the refectory by volunteers. On the way out of Winchester, towards Southampton, or as part of your walk by the river, there are alms of another kind. St Cross Hospital is the oldest almshouse in England, (formed some 400 years before the Lord Leycester at Warwick), built by Henry de Blois, William the Conqueror's grandson in 1132, where the dole of Hampshire ale and bread is still given to wayfarers at the porter's lodge. The hospital provided a home for 13 brethren, now 25, and food to 100 or more deserving people in the city. Now St Cross plans to give refreshment in the morning and afternoon, for those who enjoy taking the meadow walk to the Hospital from May to September.

Winchester Cathedral

Winchester, Hampshire SO23 9LS. Tel Visitors Centre: 01962 840471
Fax 01962 841684.
Open: daily 9.30-5. Suggested donation.
Refectory: seats 90 inside, 40 outside. Open: 9.30-5. Closed Christmas Day.
Rail: Winchester.
Bus: 1.5 mile.
Road: signposted from M3. Parking in city.

The Hospital of St Cross

St Cross, Winchester, Hampshire SO23 9SD. Tel 01962 852888

Dorchester Abbey

Oxfordshire

Foreign tourist or British townee will be heartened to discover that England is alive and well in this part of Oxfordshire. Dorchester is a really agreeable place to visit with much to see. Once again, the topography was the reason for settlement, where the River Thame and Thames met and there was a crossing point. Neolithic, Bronze and Iron Age Man, Romans and later the Normans settled here. It is difficult to imagine that Dorchester predates Winchester as an important religious centre. In 635 St Birinus, who was the Bishop of Dorchester, baptised the pagan Saxon King Cynegils, marking the beginning of Christianity in South and West England. The present church was part of a Augustinian monastery, founded in 1120, which survived the Reformation remarkably well. This is an idyllic church. The scale and quality of light recall the Suffolk wool churches for me. The most famous piece of art-work is the Jesse window, a wonderful combination of stained glass, figure sculpture and stone tracery. The church occupies a prime position and its location behind a small tollgate house, with a lych-gate and profusion of roses in the summer, is a delightful scene.

The Abbey Tea-Rooms are situated in the restored Abbey Guest House, adjoining a small museum showing the history of Dorchester. Everything that is lovable, idiosyncratic and indefatigable in English women who inspire and encourage others, is at hand in the personality of Lettice Godfrey who manages the Tea-Rooms. Twenty years ago, on her retirement, she asked the vicar if she could run a tea-room to raise money for charity. (She raised £7,000 in 1995.) She and her volunteer band of 60 or more bake, care for and beguile. Lettice makes all the jams; they change by season and sit stacked in serried ranks on the tiny kitchen shelves, waiting for us hungry tea buffs to decimate the store. The small tea-room seats 20. Visitors sit *en famille* at two tables positively groaning with scones, gooseberry cake, Dorset apple cake, chocolate, Victoria sponge and fruit cakes, as well as flapjacks and shortbread. The food, jugs of fresh roses and company inspire friendship. This is where the fun begins. As you select mouthwatering choices, everyone is asked to write down on a slate what they have eaten, while Lettice and her cohorts ply you with tea.

This is surely what going out for an English country tea epitomises; just as it was, and can still be, before the cafeteria counter culture took us over. Crab-apple jelly, gooseberry and strawberry jam are there for the taking, and the price of tea gets cheaper the more cups you imbibe! The place is simple, enlivened by the colourful tables and amusing little notices: *'Customers are exhorted not to take more butter and jam than they can eat. It is liable to render the proprietress violent'*, and *'Smokers are unwelcome and are evicted immediately'*. This tea-room is run with remarkable spirit, *con brio*. I wish we had more such engaging excursions.

You can eat enough to speed you on a pilgrimage up to Wittenham Clumps via the river and it is amazing value. A friend and I did just this, after an unforgettable tea. We had been studying the work of Paul Nash, who painted this 3,000-year-old hill fort with its clump of landmark trees. Dorchester is worth a perambulation for its fine coaching inns and houses, and the nearby village of Ewelme should also be seen. This has the oldest and most impressive grammar school in England and some exceptional almshouses built in 1437 under a licence given by Henry VII, probably the earliest example of brick used in Oxfordshire. Ewelme also has watercress beds, now up for sale. Did Ewelme and Abinger Hammer (see page 97) growers take their produce to the Watercress market in Farringdon described in Mayhew's London? This is where country looking fellows in *'smock frocks'* set out their baskets of cresses at 5am for the crowds to choose from.

Readers of Flora Thompson's *Lark Rise* trilogy, based on her childhood in the north of Oxfordshire, will know that poverty among villagers in 1880 was severe. Sometimes the only relish to put on the bread was mustard or brown sugar. She paints a picture that emphasises the seasons, and describes the high teas which eked out the products of the ubiquitous pig, which every family kept. The fortunate would eat fresh meat on Sunday but on ordinary days tea, being the main meal of the day, would include cooked fruit, a boiled jam or currant pudding to fill them up before the bacon, and cabbage. There is no doubt that fashions have changed. Every self-respecting mother tells her children that they must eat up their greens or they cannot have any pudding! In truth, the poverty that Flora Thompson describes was a kind of rough plenty. Each family grew its own vegetables, and jams, pickles and chutney were made. They cured their own bacon and many kept bees. Is it only technology that has changed

all this? *A cautionary note:* better to make your journey to Dorchester on a Wednesday or Thursday *'when summer comes in May'*. Although there is some outside seating with a view of the Abbey, queues form on a Sunday for this precious tea-room.

Dorchester Abbey

Dorchester-on-Thames, Oxfordshire OX10 7HZ.
Open: daily 9-dusk.
Tea-room in Abbey Guest House: seats 20 inside, 12 outside. Open: Sat before Easter-end Sept Wed & Thur from mid-May: sat 3-5.30.
Rail: Didcot or Reading.
Bus: from Abingdon, Oxford or Reading.
Road: A4174. Limited parking in village.

The Museum of Modern Art

Oxford

Think of Oxford and a picture of *dreaming spires* and university buildings which seem to have been there since time immemorial comes to mind. As Matthew Arnold wrote, *'Beautiful city! so venerable, so lovely.'* I never need an excuse to go there.

Oxford, originally a Saxon town, is older than the University, in which there are more than 20 colleges. The first signs of organised teaching were noted in 1133, with the first Chancellor being appointed in 1214. The magic of Oxford needs more than a two-hour visit. Better to concentrate on or combine looking at St Mary's (the University church, where preaching took place in the porch) with Christ Church, built by Cardinal Wolsey, with Grinling Gibbons carvings in the chapel and wonderful gardens. Or, choose the Bodleian Library, the Radcliffe Camera with its impressive dome, the Sheldonian Theatre, (designed by Sir Christopher Wren) and New College, founded by William Wykeham. This was designed as a self-contained building and is still unaltered, with a beautiful garden. Apart from the University buildings, the oldest architecture can be found in the churches, and there are a few gable-end houses in Pembroke Street.

The University colleges had their own special feast days. There is an Oxford and Cambridge Pudding. Gervase Markham gave a recipe for nearby Banbury cakes in 1615, and this spiced biscuit is still sold. In 1762 Parson Woodforde, diarist, gourmand, Winchester scholar and Christ Church fellow was made steward of the college, a task performed by one fellow each week of every year, as Woodforde wrote *'to see the meat of the college weighed ... taking turns each year ad infinitum'* for which he was paid 6s 6d. Woodforde enjoyed his food greatly. Christmas dinner in 1773, included *'two fine Codds with fryed souls ... oyster sauce, a fine sirloin of beef roasted, some peas soup and an orange pudding'*, the first course! The second of duck, lamb, salad and mince pies was followed by the third *'a fine plum cake'*. You are unlikely to find anyone selling mutton pies on the streets today as The Oxford Pieman, Ben Tyrell, did in 1760. But the food in the covered market, off Market Street is a worthwhile diversion. Victuals are sold by game-dealers, cheesemongers (one stall has a vast range of country cheeses), butchers, flower-sellers, bakers and fishmongers. There are bustle, colour and sounds not experienced in a clinical supermarket. Each stall has a charm and all are enclosed in a Victorian building; this spectacle can no longer be found in London.

Oxford is also a city of customs: *Beating the Bounds, Chipping the Block, and Hunting the Mallard.* The last was a feast to commemorate the building of All Souls College in 1438 when a mallard flew out of a drain on the site during the laying of the foundations. The tradition is, however, celebrated in the second year of a century, when six officers *'hunt'* the bird with staves and lanterns, singing and wearing special badges; the next is due in 2001! Let us hope that it will be a little more sober than the account of the 1801 anniversary, when the Fellows were spotted from the other side of Radcliffe Square by Bishop Heber at 4am as they walked on the college roofs with lighted torches, chorusing thunderously, *'Oh by the blood of King Edward!'* Of all the fairs once held in the City only one survives, that of St Giles.

Oxford was changed between the Wars by new industries. Already William Morris was concerned 50 years earlier: *'I wish to appeal to the mercy of the Dons to spare a few specimens of ancient town architecture ... Oxford thirty years ago, when I first knew, it was full of these treasures; but Oxford "culture" steeped to the lips in commercialism of the day, has made a clean sweep of most of them.'* Today there is a by-pass, a park-and-ride system, good rail links but Oxford is for walking.

In Pembroke Street, you will find a refreshing contrast to past history, the Museum of Modern Art which is at the cutting edge in its programming. Unlike the other museums in this book, it does not have a permanent collection. Instead, it hosts changing exhibitions of paintings, photography, video art and installation, making it a bran tub, to dip into frequently. The MOMA café is also of the dipping-in type — relaxed, informal with a mixture of sofas and low-level tables, as well as conventional dining furniture.

The ambience is distinctly 1970s and it attracts Oxford students as well as art lovers. The black-and-white decor is wearing thin in places, but frequently changing foyer exhibitions take the eye. Most food is made in a small kitchen and as there is no area to hold food, dishes are reheated as ordered; service is slick and convivial. The menu, like the exhibitions, is eclectic: thick, deep flans, (somehow mutton pies would be out of context), hot lentil loaf with tomato sauce, and creative salads — not the bland, shredded iceberg variety. Reasonably priced light dishes and excellent sandwiches give everyone a chance to eat at the museum café. A large selection of cakes and puddings includes Pavlova, upside-down apricot and chocolate, plus a choice of coffees, iced coffee, and chocolate. This café is popular and has its own food character. We need more cafés like this one in museums and galleries where food is a concern and the prices are not frightening.

Museum of Modern Art

30 Pembroke St, Oxford OX1 1BP. Tel 01865 722733 Fax 01865 722573.
Admission charge for Museum. Free access to café.
Open:Tue-Sat 10-6. Late night Thurs 9. Sun 2-6.
Café: seats 95. Open: 9-5.30, last orders 5. Late night Thurs 9. Sun 12-5.
Rail: Oxford.
Bus: many routes.
Road: A40. Park- and-ride on major approach roads.

Waterperry Gardens

Oxfordshire

Waterperry Gardens are unexpected. As one of the original students of The School of Gardening, started here in 1932, wrote it is *'a gardener's garden'*. This garden has infinite charm, and oozes tranquillity. It merits the line from Vita Sackville-West's marvellous poem *The Land*, *'This country habit has me by the heart'*.

The gardens, situated by the River Thame, are a series of pictures from a living catalogue reflecting different influences, whilst paying homage to the important gardeners in Waterperry's history. This continues today; with new developments as each garden matures so new gardens are designed. Waterperry is an all-year-round inspiration. The herbaceous border was planted without any bedding whatsoever by Beatrix Havergal who founded The School of Gardening. In winter, the geometry of the formal garden, the sculptural pear cordons and hornbeam walk give order and make this a visit of another kind. In February there are clumps of fat snowdrops in Sebbs' corner and in the walk down to the river. Seats are strategically placed to maximise the vistas. There are oaks, limes and copper beeches, one near Miss Havergal's border, another on the lawn as well as ranks of cordon fruit planting, a new rose and formal garden. These are also working gardens; fruit is grown and sold in the farm shop. The gardens surround a courtyard with a Saxon church and a restored 18th century barn now a gallery showing hand-painted textiles, ceramics and paintings by local artists.

How satisfying to find somewhere so beautiful that is open to visitors in winter when others are closed; although the high summer colour has gone, the walks are still regenerating. Vita Sackville-West's gardeners Pamela Schwerdt and Sibylle Kreutzberger whom she nicknamed *'Mädchen'*, were trained here, as was Miss Mary Spiller some 10 years later, by Miss Havergal. Although Miss Spiller is now retired, she finds it difficult to leave

Waterperry and is still very much involved with planning. She told me about the philosophy and discipline which were to prove inspirational to all who came under Miss Havergal's direction. Vita herself described the speed and efficiency of the two gardeners who carried out their tasks at Sissinghurst. Miss Havergal's teaching gave them the foundation and qualifications to build on Vita Sackville-West and Harold Nicholson's work. Women were trained here as professional gardeners, probably for the first time.

The herbaceous gardens are over 100 years old, but the house stands on the site of a former Saxon settlement. For some time it was owned by Lord Curzon. Although Waterperry House dates from the late 12th century, it was altered in both the 15th and 18th when lastly a high wall enclosed the churchyard. These changes underpin the singular nature of Waterperry now run by the School of Economic Science. The church built very near the house has a Saxon and Norman chancel, unpainted weather-boarded spire, a box pew, triple-decker pulpit and is full of early and 20th century stained glass work. The sensitively restored barn houses Arts and Crafts and links up with an 'Art in Action' exhibition every summer.

The tea-shop with a pleasing view is, however, a simple single-storey lecture room in an annexe and in no way reflects the architectural mosaic of the estate. Yet it is quite unique, as everything and by this I mean *everything* from bread to Christmas cakes, is made here. The basic counters and ambience do not do justice to the quality of the food. No matter; everyone comes for the spirit of the place and the taste. When I first saw the building my heart sank. I imagined that I would find no more than the odd portion of shrink-wrapped Cheddar or a Danish pastry. How wrong I was! All is devised to lure: fruity parsnip soup, whole-meal bread, savoury aubergine, date and almond pudding, roast lamb, good vegetables and quite amazing puddings. One is a deep redcurrant tart plus a pear and almond tart and fruit cakes as moist as you like, but without sugar. The chef uses fruit from the orchards, and they sell their own farm-pressed juices and jam.

I shopped here, just as I do elsewhere, in local markets and village shops where I am tempted to buy locally produced food. At Christmas there are puddings, this was voted best ever by my family, meringues, mincemeat, as well as bottles of Russet and Cox's apple juice, with incomparable taste. You will be lucky to find cakes and puddings like this anywhere outside London which are made by their own Swiss pâtissier. What a find!

This is not a sophisticated tea-room but one where you eat well and leave feeling spoiled. It is the antithesis of a standardised

 motorway pit-stop and, although the manage-ment hope gradually to upgrade the service counters and kitchens, they are adamant that they will maintain the personal attention, the quality of the food and the spirit of the place which are, after all, the magnet.

Waterperry Gardens

Waterperry, nr Wheatley, Oxfordshire OX33 1JZ. Tel 01844 339254 Fax 01844 339883.
Open: March-Oct: 10-5.30 weekdays, 10-6 weekends. Nov-Feb: 10-5.
Admission charge for gardens, reduced in winter.
Tea-room: seats 80 inside, 80 outside, same hours. Free access.
Rail: Thame/Haddenham Parkway, then bus to Wheatley 2.5 miles.
Bus: Country bus from Aylesbury or Oxford.
Road: A40. Easy parking.

Buckinghamshire

Middlescx

Northamptonshire

Suffolk

Warwickshire

Chenies Manor

Buckinghamshire

Chenies village and Manor make an attractive excursion; the village is a backwater surprisingly not far from the omnipresent M25, in green-belt country. Chenies Manor was originally a 15th century hall house and is still a working farm, with a Tudor house, and characteristic landmark chimneys; it has its own chapel, substantial farm buildings, and quite delightful cottage gardens. There are 4000 tulips in early May and even at the end of October the intense colour of the dahlias illuminated the misty afternoon.

A successful marriage between a daughter of the Cheney family with Sir John Russell, the first Earl of Bedford, in 1523, advanced the expansion of the house, from the earlier tower and hall. The south wing with its line of magnificent Tudor chimneys is the largest addition dating from 1529. These developments confirm Sir John's political standing and the necessity of entertaining the sovereign; Elizabeth I and Henry VIII stayed frequently. Alistair Macleod Matthews told me that when Nikolaus Pevsner visited this house he called it a *'conundrum'* — it is indeed a mixture of several styles and ages; most predominant are 17th century square-cut gable ends and the chimneys. The church just outside the walls can be seen. Although the Bedford chapel has the best monumental statuary of any parish church, it is not open to the public. Chenies remained with the Russell family, who own Woburn, until 1953, and has since been the home of the Macleod Matthews who provide a wonderful welcome.

Most of Chenies village was built and developed by the Russell family between the 1820s and 1860s in the Elizabethan revival style; it could have been designed by Edward Blore, or was possibly based on a pattern which was used for the estate cottages at Woburn or, as you might see, for example, at Edensor near Chatsworth. It has a charm in its design and plan, being set around a village green, complete with well, adjoining the surrounding walls of the Manor House. This village is virtually untouched and this illustrates the importance that constant management can have in safeguarding such an architectural entity. A thriving local conservation society continues this cause.

The house is unexpectedly light. Many rooms have a double aspect and the pervading friendliness owes much to the human scale, the warmth of the brick, and the elements of the different sunken gardens. On one visit there was a special spooky tour to mark Hallowe'en, but the gardens themselves are spellbinding in another way. Visitors are shown the whole house: Tudor hall, priest's hole, privy, dining room decorated in 1820 in Regency style, and all the family rooms, one with an enchanting collection of antique dolls. Delightful 17th and 18th century furniture and textiles and Louis XVI furniture are the attraction; this is a family house with a mixture of furniture and fashions for everyone. Several rooms were decorated with William Morris wallpaper in the 1880s; the red bedroom is particularly appealing. Different generations have put in a variety of floors in pine and oak, contributing to the bright atmosphere. All the rooms give wonderful views of the gardens, fields and the church.

I am not usually excited by the prospect of tea-rooms in barns, but this is a far cry from the neglected, one bunch-of-driedflowers variety seen all too often. The Chenies barn was built in 1812 and has been sympathetically furnished and restored with the help of local craftsmen. There is warmth, care and an agreeable welcome, no plastic but rather an Arts and Crafts character with typical lighting, textiles and oak furniture. Wherever you sit there is a view onto the gardens. And as for dried flowers, there is a cornucopia of colour and cultivars, all picked by local friends using the fruits and spoils of the garden. The drying process in the loft of another barn near the shop, is part of the tour. Wisely they keep the tea simple. A large table of good plump cakes is set out invitingly; we could have fruit cake or sponges and small biscuits. The prices suit families with ravening tribes of children on a half-term treat. Only the scones come from the bakers, the rest are made by friends and well-wishers. The setting is congenial and invites conversation. There is such a relaxed, sociable, atmosphere among the visitors taking refreshment in the tea-room which surely comes only with a personal interest not always conspicuous at other historical sites. It is at Chenies.

Chenies is situated in the middle of good walking country which is well signposted. One walk which runs along the valley, by the River Chess, at the foot of the Chilterns, is well marked with public footpaths in the meadows. And from the House a path takes a steep drop to Latymer, past a mill parts of which are even older than the Manor.

Chenies Manor

Chenies, Rickmansworth, Herts WD3 6ER. Tel 01494 762888.
House and tea-room open: April-end Oct 2-5 Wed, Thurs and BH Mon.
Admission charge.
Tube and rail: Chorleywood from Baker Street or Marylebone.
Bus: 336 from Watford to Amersham, 1.5 miles.
Road: J18 M25. Parking nearby.

Waddesdon Manor

Buckinghamshire

W*hat a House!'* wrote James Lees Milne, instrumental in setting up The National Trust's historic house acquisition policy, when he first saw Waddesdon in 1947. It is an extraordinary experience and its complexities require far more space than this piece can justify. After driving up a wooded and beautifully curving drive, cradled in hills, you are confronted by a château-like, but, in effect, late Victorian mansion in deep golden Bath stone. This is Chambord in the Chilterns, complete with playing fountains. The Victorian exterior belies the ornate interior wherein all is 17th and 18th century France, an opulence not matched anywhere outside France.

Waddesdon was built between 1874 and 1889 by Baron Ferdinand de Rothschild, who had lived in England since he was 21. He was the grandson of the Austrian line of Rothschilds the banking family which began in Frankfurt in the 18th century and founded dynasties throughout Europe. This house, designed by G. H. Destailleur, is the consequence of many French influences, architecture, turrets, accentuated Mansard roofs; magnificent furniture, decorative arts and gardens by Elie Lainé. The collections are glittering and reflect the intimacy that the Rothschild family held with the French royal family. The presentation is exquisite, showing the combination of objects and textiles that would have been seen in France, yet housed to reflect the style of a Victorian country house. The Baron wanted to live in the comfort of a Victorian landowner, surrounded by his magnificent *'objets d'art'*. Whilst one member of the family said, *'the couches and satin cushions, and palms and photos of crowned heads with autograph signatures was a never ending source of pleasure'*, Gladstone's daughter Mary was not so impressed; she wrote: *'I felt much oppressed with the extreme gorgeousness and luxury'*. You need to enter this house with a different mindset to visiting English Country houses to appreciate its exceptional character. The features that imbue the interior are the *'boiseries'*, essentially carved oak, which give Waddesdon its singular sense of being in another place — France. These wood panels, taken from French town houses or hotels pulled down during the modernisation of Paris by Baron Haussman in the 1860s, date from the 17th and 18th century. They have become the intrinsic fabric of many rooms. The decoration of the billiard room, in England usually oak or mahogany, is panelled here with 18th century walnut, but the *'boiseries'* in the Green Boudoir have a more exotic jewel-like quality. As in so many others this room has a beautiful Savonnerie carpet, similar to several woven for the French royal family. The cabinets, tables, chairs (some used by Louis XV) and the Sèvres porcelain, which has recently been dramatically re-displayed, are the essence of 18th century French taste. However the Baron's love of his 'adopted' England is reflected in the beautiful English portraits of the 18th century by Sir Joshua Reynolds and Sir Thomas Gainsborough. Waddesdon demands careful viewing, looking up and down to avoid missing any of the treasures. I suggest revisiting.

The facilities in such a perfect setting could not copy but should compliment. And sensibly, the panelled rooms of the servants' wing are not embellished; this is the visitors' dining area. An old kitchen, complete with ceiling-height dresser, iron stove canopy and full of copper utensils reminds me of my early training at a hotel school. Although the space is worthy of a better bar, reflecting the quality of the craftsmanship elsewhere, there is no sense of being below stairs, with the view of the main drive and the park beyond.

These rooms were part of the large servants' wing needed to accommodate the number of staff to satisfy the comfort and scale of Victorian living and entertaining. There were five kitchens, a servants' room, steward's and housekeeper's room and a still room, a legacy from medieval houses where ladies of the house, not allowed into the kitchens, distilled their cordials and sweet delicacies. Still rooms later became the area for preparing tea and other beverages. Elsewhere Waddesdon followed the 'rules' or etiquette of design for Victorian living, laid down by the architect Robert Kerr, in the family apartments where the bachelors wing was designed to keep the sexes separate. However, at Waddesdon today's visitors enter the house through the main doors, just as visitors would have been received. The planning for their enjoyment is outstanding.

There is no patronising terminology on the menu, no *'servants' hall soup'* or other irritants, although Waddesdon provides the opportunity to milk cultural connections in food. Pleasing to see home-cooked ham and farmhouse cheeses, and sensible casseroles and fish, any of which can be washed down with a bottle of Rothschild's estate bottled Château Lafite at exceptional value. At least 12 different cakes are set out on the dresser, albeit clingfilmed. Choices abound, and the food is excellent value. As it opens right up to Christmas, Waddesdon unquestionably makes an enticing place to eat and shop.

Queen Victoria visited only once; the menu for her visit in 1890 included six courses, from potages to entremets; the order of the menu shows the changes that have taken place; the fashion of eating asparagus as an entremets *à la Française* has been reversed, more often this is a first course. The Queen was offered among others consommé à la Windsor, Truite à la Norvégienne, and Caneton aux Ortolans, an entrée, a rôti and a soufflé. It is recorded that she enjoyed the occasion and sent the Baron a statue as an expression of her pleasure. The gardens, designed by the French landscape artist Lainé, harmonise with the house and are open almost all year. Baron Ferdinand supervised the planting and the whole effect, aviary, sculpture and planning of formal areas, is one of only three 19th century gardens now in the care of the National Trust, influenced by the French style.

Waddesdon champions its own character throughout the visit, from glittering house to cool contrasting wine cellars where *premiers crus* are laid down by the owners of the most celebrated vineyards in the world.

Waddesdon Manor

Waddesdon, nr Aylesbury, Buckinghamshire HP18 OJH. Tel 01296 651282
Fax 01296 651293.
Open: end March to end of Oct. Thurs-Sun 12.30-6.
Admission charge. Free to NT members.
Restaurant: seats 100. Open: end of Feb-Dec 22.
Stables tea-room open: BH, Good Friday and weekends.
Admission charge for garden and tea-room.
Rail: Aylesbury.
Bus: 5 miles from Aylesbury.
Road: A41.

Osterley Park

Middlesex

Osterley Park is definitely *rus in urbe*. It imparts a feeling of being on a large estate, yet it is at the very edge of central London. Of the original *'fair and stately house of brick'* built by Sir Thomas Gresham in 1577 only the stable block remains. Sir Thomas was a wealthy man who founded the Royal Exchange and built other country houses for himself.

In 1683 the house was sold to Nicholas Barbon, the first speculative builder who contributed to the changes and scale of housing in London, aspired to reach the same heights as Gresham and to live in the same manner. Barbon added the Tuscan columns and large, impressive door to the stable block, and the horse stalls. Later a dairy was added, where one visitor was *'taken with the milk pails and butter tubs with brass mounts gleaming with gold, and Chinese bowls laid out on grey marble'*. In 1782 another visitor described one of the many Chinese summer houses as being *'arranged in the taste and custom of the country'* and set out as *'The tea-room in the garden'*. What a superb scene these pictures evoke, but alas are no longer to be seen.

The house was transformed in 1761 by Robert Adam, the great architect whose command of classical architecture is used here with spirit. It is with Adam and his approach that this house is synonymous. Having already worked at Hatchlands and newly arrived on the London scene, he was commissioned by the then owner Sir Francis Child to bring order to the unplanned additions that had taken place over the previous years. The image of the house that I and, I imagine, most visitors will remember, is that of the four turrets, which are original, and the graceful portico added by Adam. The results won praise from Horace Walpole who described the outcome as being a *'palace of palaces'*. For connoisseurs of the Neo-Classical style, it is a pilgrimage.

Adam brought his knowledge of antiquity but also his vitality and desire to change the prevailing attitude towards *'the elegant art of interior decoration'*. First he built the impressive transparent double portico and raised the courtyard to rationalise the route up the existing steps and provide a more important entrance. The elegant Hall is skilfully lengthened with semicircular niches at each end containing statues. This became the principal room for receptions and was occasionally used for eating. As the kitchens were some distance away, Adam designed a counter behind the door leading to the servants' staircase to make the service of food easier. The drawings for this Hall can be seen at the Victoria and Albert Museum, and many hundreds more are kept by the Sir John Soane Museum.

The Etruscan Room, the Eating Room, and the Library, are all Adam's work. His great staircase has a screen of columns and the stucco work on the walls symbolises hospitality with panels of vases and ewers; the decoration becomes more ornate as you ascend. This is not simply an Adam treatment of the earlier building. The interior has been imbued with his singular ordered style. The panels, pier glass, ceilings, furniture and carpets were all designed because Adam wished to incorporate art into architecture. Elsewhere the Adam signature, stucco, is a triumph. In the Eating Room a profusion of grapes, ivy and other Bacchanalian motifs are the appropriate decoration. And there is more; a theatrical state bed, a golden-yellow Breakfast Room and a Long Gallery. All are perfectly sumptuous.

Robert Adam was holistic in his planning so it is not surprising to read that he had strong views on the design and function of eating rooms. He considered the main difference in decoration between the French and English was in attitude and customs. The French did not consider decoration important in the dining rooms, where they met only for dining, so the display of food became the '*show*'; conversely, he believed that the English, because of our climate, were inclined towards the bottle, as well as to conversation and political discussion. This directed him to advise that eating rooms should be fitted in a different style to other rooms. In preference to damask hangings, he wrote that '*they should be finished with stucco, and ordained with statues and paintings, that they may not retain the smell of victuals*'. At Osterley you will find such decoration. Codes of conduct for the time in these rooms were advanced in *The honours of the table* written in 1788, by John Trusler, in which rigid rules of etiquette were laid down for the order of arrival in the dining room; ladies entered first, with the most important lady guest next to the mistress of the house, followed by the male guests seated in similar rank. Shortly after this the fashion of seating ladies alternately with men, still maintained today, was adopted.

The park at Osterley, unlike many other historic houses, is open throughout the year and the faithful locals that I saw on the last opening day of 1995, a cold and crisp Sunday before Christmas, would dearly like the tea-room to stay open too. It is very popular with walkers and young families, so this is an important West London lung as well as a pleasure ground.

The tea-room is located in the original 16th century stables next to the house. The façade is not ornate, but the contrast of Tudor brick, windows and massive door make it exceptional. No order or fashion for seating, but the tea-room is divided by different levels and type of seating; an uneven cobbled floor in the horse stall area has refectory tables and benches, while the lower area has tables with printed cloth and metal chairs. These latter-day items do not reflect any of this architectural history; more oak furniture would not be amiss but the building is very much part of the fabric and social history. The food is straightforward and all made in the small kitchen behind the counter. Furthermore, the friendly staff take pride in the food that they prepare, welcome you and are prepared to discuss their dishes. In summer, flowers for the tea-room and the house are gathered from the garden behind the stables, and visitors can enjoy their refreshment outside in a lovely walled garden during fine weather.

After a good walk, the soup with a roll, the only item not made here, is just what is needed; hot and lightly spiced lentil and tomato soup is cheering. The cakes are good, and good value; they sit on the counter, not parsimoniously plated. You can choose from at least five, which include date and walnut, Victoria sponge and a chocolate biscuit cake. That perennial, cream tea, is excellent value. There are light lunches. And I thought their

 special choice and portions for children showed an understanding of their needs. They will provide small portions of soup and salad, if asked. On the way home take time to visit the estate farm shop, which supplies the vegetables for the tea-room, where you can buy vegetables, eggs and hay if you have a horse, or even a guinea-pig!

Osterley Park

Isleworth, Middlesex TW7 4RB. Tel 0181 5603918 Fax 0181 7582116.
Open: Wed-Sun 1-5 end of March - end Oct. BH 11-5.
Admission charge to House. Free to NT members.
Tea-room: seats 56 inside, 63 in garden. Wed-Sun 11.30-5 end of March-end Oct
and BH. Nov and Dec Sat and Sun 12-4. Tel 0181 569 7624.
Tube: Osterley.
Bus: 110, 111, 120, H91.
Road: A4. Parking 220 yards and courtesy car.

Coton Manor Garden

Northamptonshire

I nevitably I arrive at houses situated in the middle of the country on a quiet day, often at the end of the season, and sometimes on a Friday. This is the acid test or taste test for a restaurant in a historic site or museum. All these factors were in place, but my luck was in. If management can get it right on a dismal day, there is no doubt that on delightful summer days, when they are busier, things will go swimmingly.

Northamptonshire, which calls itself the Rose of the Shires, is in some areas more of the 19th than the 20th century. This is one my own favourite counties. I like the mellow limestone, the roofs of mossy stone Colley Weston slate that you find in many of the villages. I like the churches, especially Brixworth which is the oldest and most intact Saxon church in England. In this county there are still pockets of peace where I can escape the motorways, stay in and find unspoilt country, and even pick up asparagus sold in the field. Away from towns it is a quiet and unpretentious region. Daniel Defoe in his *Tour thro' the Whole Island of Great Britain* described Northampton as *'the handsomest and best built town in this part of the country'*. This is, I suppose, the southern end of the heart of England; nearby the battle of Naseby took place when this village was razed to the ground by Cromwell's troops. The county of Northamptonshire used to celebrate the Restoration until the 1950s when children in villages wore sprigs of oak leaf and carried bunches of nettles which they used to attack anyone who was not sporting the oak!

Coton Manor is a farmhouse built in 1662. It has been altered over the last 300 years but lived in by the present family for three generations. The house, however, is not open, the garden is the attraction. This was laid out in the 1920s, when the farm was altered to make land available for the terraces, pond, yew hedges and herbaceous borders.

All three generations of the family have contributed to this garden, where plants are propagated and sold. I bought another lavender plant for the bees on my allotment. The garden is planned to offer colour all through the opening season. Changes in levels and planting afford places to relax, to gaze out from and to wander through. The water garden is surrounded by a backdrop of willows, cherry, plum and silver birch. There are scented rhododendrums, and in the shady spot hellebores and ferns, whilst primulas and bluebells are out in the spring. This is a charming location, where the sound of water encourages dallying and relaxation.

In the restaurant, situated in a small courtyard, a pleasant young waitress greeted me, and a jug of water was automatically put on the table, quite unusually. And I found another surprise here. The furniture, pictures and crockery (white and green) had all been thoughtfully chosen to reflect the place and the history, in a sensitive but not contrived manner. The owners have a good eye for detail. I enjoyed the substantial leek and potato soup and the yeasty bread, made by a Norwegian lady who lives in the village — an unbelievable contrast to the pre-baked, reheated roll I would have had to make do with if I had stopped on a motorway. Coton supports Moulton, the nearby agricultural college, buying ice-cream that is made by the students.

The afternoon teas include homemade scones, traditional sponges, coffee, lemon and chocolate cake. There are set teas, with cucumber sandwiches, at an inclusive price. Unusually it opens in the evening on Fridays and Saturdays, as well as Sunday lunch throughout the year when a seasonal game casserole and Coton's own specially made ginger ice-cream are some of the dishes from a small individual menu. Booking is essential for evenings and Sundays, but the bill for two or three courses will not break the bank. Coton is not only a spot which requires several visits, but also deserves to thrive because it so obviously cares about the spirit of the gardens and the comfort and enjoyment of its visitors. There is a generosity which is engendered by the family working in the garden and constantly planning anew. They are now considering a wild flower meadow, another bonus for the world-weary visitor.

Coton Manor Garden

nr Guilsborough, Northampton, Northamptonshire NN6 8RQ. Tel 0604 740219 Fax 01604 740838.
Garden open: Easter to Sept Wed - Sun and BH12-5.30.
Admission charge.
Restaurant: seats 50. Open as Garden.
Free access.
Rail: Long Buckby 4 miles, Northampton 9 miles.
Bus: from Northampton and 1 mile walk.
Road: A428 and A50. Parking: on the spot.

The Guildhall

Lavenham, Suffolk

Lavenham is exceptional, a small town where you have to raise your eyes, for the most decorative and interesting features are often at first floor level and above. All the buildings would have been related to wool and their design is a conspicuous display of wealth. Although the wool trade has disappeared, the town still lives and shines.

The Guildhall is worth a special expedition. It was acquired by The National Trust in 1951, having already become one of the first buildings to attract the attention of SPAB, the Society for the Protection of Ancient Buildings, in the 1880s but the whole town walk deserves time. Like many of the other Suffolk wool churches, St Peter and St Paul owes its existence and quality to a wool merchant's gift, that of the Spring family. The limestone was brought from Lincolnshire and Northamptonshire and mixed with local flint. I like Lavenham in the late autumn when the colours of plaster wash, deep pink, and timbers are uplifting; here the timbers are not stained so the effect is mellow.

In the 16th century under Henry VIII, Lavenham was fourteenth in a list of the most wealthy towns in England producing cloth called Lavenham Blue. Thankfully today, some of the small factories built in the 19th and 20th century survived, one houses Lavenham's own printing press. John Constable attended the Grammar School, which has some of the town's most impressive interior carvings in the form of an angel frieze.

I love the timber houses, the decorative pargeting, raised plasterwork, and the row of small shops opposite the Guildhall. I am told that some visitors are so keen to photograph the whole scene without any cars that they can be seen at a very early hour around the Market Square taking their pictures. Of course this square would have been the hub, with a charter market for animals and produce licensed since 1257. There are several shops, but you will not find any supermarkets here; no good for those who need that kind of fix! You will, however, find a secondhand book shop in Water Street near the Swan hotel, antique dealers, a baker's, greengrocer's, butcher's and grocery, and artists who sell their pictures and crafts. One house in the square has a rarely seen golden *'Hovis'* sign. It is a treat to use these shops. As long as residents and visitors shop here and it is prevented from becoming just a quick stop for coaches which would, inevitably, alter the balance towards gift shops, the integrity, scale and joy of this town should survive.

There is no need for any façade or make believe in Lavenham which is the real thing. Alec Clifton-Taylor numbered the Guildhall among those buildings which delighted him. Who would disagree? It is magnificent; you could almost say over-timbered, with beautiful hand-made roof tiles. The contrast of the lime plaster filling between the silver oak of the timbers, is dazzling. Carvings on the corners, around the ground floor entrance of the double porch and all along the first floor bressumer, the overhanging beam which runs along the whole length of the building, are quite ornate. Guildhalls were not just the result of successful trade but guilds also provided associations and support for their members. They set out trading rules, standards of quality and ensured that proper wages were paid to all their craftsmen members.

Readers will have gathered that I liked connections. This one is a gem. Amongst its many uses the Guildhall housed evacuees in the war and, a British Restaurant. These were government-planned restaurants set up all over the country to ensure the populace had access to good food. Committees were developed to advise on both their design and management. Many were opened in similar interesting and historic sites, one in the Bethnal Green

Museum in East London. I have recently begun researching this fascinating element of the Second World War.

Today the Guildhall doubles up as a meeting place and museum. The tea-room is located at one end with its own separate entrance. This is a very pleasant place to stop in your perambulations and has a view of the garden. Service is from a tiny bar and the simple menu is good. Copella apple juice, made at nearby Boxford, is on offer and the cakes made in a minute kitchen, some with oil, are excellent value. Sadly no Suffolk bakery: no

Apple Hoggins or God's Kitchels, as baked at Christmas, and I am less enthusiastic about the rather unnecessary Victorian hand in the lace table cloths, not fitting this medieval space. Nevertheless I am always welcomed, children are cared for and even better there are no trite names on the menu.

The Guildhall of Corpus Christi

Market Place, Lavenham, Sudbury, Suffolk CO10 9QZ. Tel 01787 247646.
Open: Easter to end of Oct 11-5 daily.
Telephone for details of late Autumn opening.
Admission charge, first two children free. Free to NT members.
Free access to tea-room. Telephone for opening days.
Rail: Sudbury.
Bus: Bury St Edmunds. From Colchester on Sun only.
Road: A1141 and B1071.

Lord Leycester Hospital

Warwick

Warwick was a perfect excursion for us as children in the 1950s. It was near Leicester, where we lived, and it has a stunning castle. There were tea-shops, and still that enchanting mix of Georgian brick, some wide tree-lined streets and some narrow with black-and-white houses with the look of other days. All this, and Anne Hathaway's cottage at nearby Stratford upon Avon, captivated me at an early age. I still, inveterate tourist, have a collection of half size 1950s postcards showing the Memorial Theatre and Shakespeare's birthplace. Warwick is not only at the centre of England, it *is* England. This is a walled medieval town; it needs to be discovered on foot.

Notwithstanding a shopping precinct and a small one-way system, the rest — the marketplace and St Mary's Church (the road runs under this as you enter) — are intact. The position of the Castle and the Great Hall looking down on the River Avon is a triumph. My paean, however, is not to the Castle but to the Lord Leycester Hospital, arguably the most interesting building in the town, which opens to visitors.

In 1540 Thomas Oken persuaded the burgesses to buy the Guildhall after the reformation. It was then acquired by Robert Dudley, Earl of Leicester, who turned it into a Hospital for wounded soldiers in 1571. The Hospital abuts the West Gate, from which runs a range of medieval buildings with Victorian additions. The Hospital still houses war pensioners and there are places for 12 Brethren and their wives. I consider it to be the jewel in Warwick's architectural crown, of which the burgesses should be justly proud. It deserves better directional signs. There are few signs to guide you here.

Several rooms run round three sides of a galleried courtyard. The timbers, very wide, in the Great Hall, and the decorative timbers (oak between cream lime wash) outside are quite special.

The friendly Brethren sell tickets, guide books, postcards and talk about the regimental Museum, or whatever takes your eye or curiosity. They have time to talk; this makes the visit distinctive. On my recent visit I learned from the Master that the courtyard had been used for the BBC production of *Pride and Prejudice*. The galleried courtyard was transformed into the Strand in London where Mr Darcy seeks the runaways Lydia and Mr Wyckham. When I saw the episode on television I was pleased to have known in advance, and even more pleased for the Hospital; it must have brought some welcome income. Surely Jane Austen would not have disapproved of this transposition; she had visited Warwick, Kenilworth and Stoneleigh Abbey. Kenilworth may well be the foundation of *Northanger Abbey*, that most delightful 'Gothic' novel.

In 1806 Jane Austen's mother wrote of their stay at Stoneleigh Abbey, which had been in the Austen family for many years, an amazing house with chapel, where one servant's duties were solely baking and brewing. Their breakfast, after prayers, included '*chocolate, coffee, tea, plum cake, pound cake, hot rolls, bread and butter*'. Mrs Austen had dry toast. She also described the dairy '*where is made butter, good Warwickshire cheese, and cream ditto*'. It was so well kept, that she added '*were you to cut a finger I do not think you could find a cobweb to wrap it up in*'!

The gardens are at least 500 years old. They are now being restored in a scholarly fashion and a small pineapple pit has recently been discovered. The Gardens were mentioned in the sale

of 1540 and have been opened as part of the tour since the mid-19th century. A large stone vase called the Nilometer which may have been brought back from a Grand Tour still has to receive provenance. But the exceptional standing of this building as a place to be visited is confirmed by the detailed records of past visitors. The Hospital attracted the American writer Nathaniel Hawthorne in the early 19th century who based at least one of his novels on the experience, and was also visited by Oscar Wilde.

The tea-room at Lord Leycester Hospital is called the Brethren's Kitchen, and looks onto the courtyard. It is personalised with red checked cloths, cushions and place mats but the oak refectory tables, settles, dresser and medieval wall painting are authentic. The food is good and visitors return. The menu is also of other days' variety — I do not recall seeing herrings on toast in a tea-room since I was a child. There are other light hot snacks and proper dishes such as chicken casserole, served in a refreshingly friendly manner from a minuscule kitchen, which is on view. Apple cake, strudel and fruit loaf and very good shortbread are all made by the manager. This is surely a place that needs to be cosseted and conserved, as does Warwick itself.

Lord Leycester Hospital

High Street, Warwick, Warwickshire LV34 4BH. Tel 01926 492797 or 491422.
Admission charge, concessions.
Open: winter 10-4, March-Oct 10-5.30 Tues-Sun incl.
Tea-room: seats 30. Open: early April- end Oct 10-4.30.
Rail: Warwick.
Bus: from Stratford and Leamington Spa.
Road: A41 or M40. Own car park.

London

British Museum

What can be written about the British Museum in a short space that could possibly do justice to such a world renowned institution? It is virtually a city state of culture worthy of a two week excursion. It attracts the largest audience of any other similar institution in the world, and its name instantly conjures a image of authority. I prefer quick dips rather than sustained immersions!

The Museum is a temple of arts and history, a chronicle of antiquities, of earlier civilisations: Egyptian, Bronze Age, Etruscan, Greek, Roman and medieval and all free. It is marvellous that the multitudes, 6,000,000 a year, still flock here, as they did when it first opened 150 years ago and the numbers of *'ordinary people'*, gave the trustees concern.

This Museum originated from an earlier idea, the 17th Century *'cabinet of curiosities'*. These were private collections of such objects and specification, as fish, art and even food. The British Museum, founded in 1753, opened to the public in 1759 in Montague House in semi-rural Bloomsbury and was later rebuilt in the classical tradition in 1827 on the same site. It is a purpose-built powerhouse of archaeology, in Greek Revival style of which Pevsner wrote *'it is among the best examples in Britain, or would be if the front and grand Ionic order ... could be seen from a distance'*. A fitting design by Robert Smirke makes this the largest Neo-Classical building in the British Isles.

The BM owes its existence to the farsightedness of Sir Hans Sloane who offered his collection on the nation's behalf to King George II for £20,000 *'for the use and improvement of physic and other arts and sciences'*. It was proposed that the funds needed to buy the collection might be raised by lottery which in fact provided £95,194 8s 2d. The British Museum has an unmatched collection of porcelain and sculpture and you will find some paintings of

Turner and 20th century artists including Henry Moore.

The museum maintains a continuing programme of exhibitions, some small, which may show objects not previously seen. In the recent *Westminster Kings* architecture, history and a long lost ewer used by Richard II, since discovered in Africa, were brought together. As for large exhibitions, those who queued with excitement and expectation for the Tutankhamun exhibition in 1972 could ever forget that never-to-be-repeated experience. The awe-inspiring collections are almost too much of a feast.

There is a connection here with Baron Ferdinand de Rothschild who donated the Waddesdon bequest. He became a trustee of the Museum in 1896, but died two years later. Rothschild bequeathed an excellent collection which contains brilliant jewels and, among others, an exquisitely detailed Roman agate vase and Venetian turquoise glass. This little room or *Schatzkammer* is like a jewel case opened up to show off its contents reflecting the taste of this exceptional collector. On one visit I noticed Mrs Kipling's name on the list of benefactors of the Museum in 1939. Her husband Rudyard bought Batemans which we shall find in Sussex (see page 80).

After this visual food, you need physical refreshment. *'I had to have a cup of tea or perish'* wrote H. J. Massingham, in 1933 when searching for an elusive carving. In such situations restaurants have a tough time coping with hordes and presenting food that has to compete against some of the most beautiful objects and images the eye could ever wish to see. If more caterers grasped this point perhaps there would be more complete excursions. No danger here, the food is displayed to tempt. Salads are colourful, textural and generously displayed in large bowls. Dishes of avocado with ratatouille are planned for colour and season; roast lamb, and grilled chicken with lentil and pesto were part of the cold collation set out with care and artistry. The *'garni'* syndrome is absent. There are bubbling dishes of good stews and soup and bread is cut thickly. Cakes which seduce include fruit, lemon and chocolate truffle.

The design is modernist: white walls, golden wood furniture and glass, relieved with another dimension, a copy of a classical relief in plaster. There are two seating levels; a gallery runs around the whole space, breaking it up and adding warmth. Unusually the complete menu is on offer until 5 pm and beyond. This was like manna from heaven one Sunday afternoon when I had been hunting food at other museums in London, but just what you would expect to find in a large museum serving the world. For those who just want that *'cup of tea or perish'* and a sandwich or slice of cake, there is a coffee-shop next door.

The BM has recently won £30,000,000 from today's lottery to increase the public spaces and transform the court around the Reading Room into a piazza, justly deserved. May its wonders continue to be free for all to see.

The British Museum

Great Russell Street, London WC1B 3DG. Tel 0171 636 1555 Fax 0171 323 8118.
Open: Mon-Sat 10-5, Sun 2.30-6.
Closed: Jan 1st and Good Friday, early May BH, Dec 24-26 incl.
No admission charge.
Restaurant: seats 190, café 85.
Open: Mon-Sat 10-4.30, Sun 2.30-5.30.
Rail: Euston or King's Cross.
Tube: Holborn, Tottenham Court Road, Russell Square, Goodge Street.
Bus: 1, 7 (to door), 8, 10, 19, 22B, 24, 25, 38, 98.

Kensington Palace

We have to thank William and Mary for their attitude to commissioning architecture and their influence on garden design. It was their patronage that enabled Sir Christopher Wren to rebuild so much of London after the Great Fire, including hospitals, palaces and churches: St Paul's and at least 50 more. The manifestation of their style is proclaimed at Kensington Palace, and also in the additions they made to Hampton Court Palace, Greenwich Palace and the Royal Hospital at Chelsea. William and Mary both liked Kensington Palace; although it did not have the scale of their Dutch palace at Het Loo the air was infinitely purer than the fetid humours and crowds of the court at Whitehall which aggravated William's asthma. They both preferred the situation to Greenwich and Hampton Court which were too far away from the court. How convenient that William's secretary, the Earl of Nottingham, was prepared to sell Holland House, which Wren then made into a suitable royal residence.

Kensington Palace is a classic building in red brick with Portland stone dressings and much wood inside, *'Dutchly formal'* as Massingham wrote. Wren added four wings to old Nottingham House, with four pavilions at the corners, and made the entrance on the west side, with portico and courtyard. £100,000 was spent on changing the house; records show rates of pay for the carpenters as either 3*s* or 2*s* 8*d* per day. £11,000 was spent on the gardens which covered 26 acres. A few years later, when the gardens were completed John Evelyn wrote *'The house is very noble, the galleries furnished with all the best Pictures of all the Houses ... the Gardens about it are very delicious'*. The outcome, according to Evelyn in 1690, was *'a very sweete villa'*, rather than a Palace.

The Orangery was built in 1703 by Mary's sister Queen Anne for her own use *'where beauty herself might sip tea'*. Today this is a public space and there are few other opportunities in London to sit in a building of such quality. What was called Anne's state-ly *'Green House'*, became a green salon where she could indulge in gardening, and entertain guests to tea and supper parties. Here, among the lemon trees, the sound of music would float down from one end of the room to divert and entertain the assembly. There were possibly two hands in the planning of the marvellous building; it is thought that although the original designs by Sir John Vanbrugh were approved by Queen Anne, it is likely that Nicholas Hawksmoor oversaw the building work and made some changes. The carvings on the panelling attributed to Grinling Gibbons make this a superb space. Queen Anne also modified the gardens, widening and converting them to a more English style than that of her brother-in-law William, replacing formal box-hedged planting with flowers.

Today's Orangery tea-room is formal, elegant and ultra white. Here the scent of orange blossom dispels the gloom of a windswept January morning, and in summer provides a refuge from the London crowds. I find this pure delectation — the large, calm space, although slightly chilly in winter, is punctuated alter-nately with the fruit and bay trees. Except for the statuary in niches, nothing is allowed to interfere with the architecture, order, and majesty of the full length windows. It deserves to be described as one of the most *'beautiful examples of the art of the Renaissance in London, if not in the country'*. Today the state apartments are open to the public, where the court dress collection and a rich assem-bly of pictures by van Dyck and Tintoretto can be seen.

William and Mary wanted not only to improve their palaces but also the morals and manners of the society they had joined. As for manners in the Orangery, the food is brought to the table quite correctly. Soup with herb scones and hot casseroles are excellent value. Although a large sandwich plate is more costly, this is not a normal park pavilion and the quality of the food, especially the cakes, served on blue and white china, is excellent.

I was told a charming story by one of the waiters. An elderly gentleman who lives nearby walks here every day, and if he misses a day they telephone to enquire after him. He prefers his own blend of coffee, which they make up into a pot and he buys a pastry to accompany it.

That indefatigable diarist Parson Woodforde took time to visit the gardens on one of his excursions to London from Norwich and Bath in 1786 with his sister and brother-in-law. He tells us that on June 25th they took a coach to Kensington Gardens where they walked until 3 in the afternoon. On the walk back, to Charing Cross, *'we called at a house and refreshed ourselves with Rum and Water and then walked on'*. Turnpike and coach, cost 1*s*6*d* as did the refreshment. Fine fortification for a fair walk. How splendid that visitors and locals should still be able to take tea here and enjoy this building, almost 300 years after it was built.

Kensington Palace

State Apartments, London W8 4PX. Tel 0171 937 9561 (recorded message) Fax. 0171 376 0198.
Apartments open: daily 9.30-5 beginning May-End of Sept. Last tour 3.30. Admission charge.
Orangery: seats 80. Open:10-5. Free access.
Tube: High St, Kensington, Queensway, Bayswater.
Bus: 9, 9a, 10, 12, 49, 52, 52a, 70, 94.

Museum of Mankind

6 Burlington Gardens, London W1

Close to the Royal Academy, via an elegant walk through Burlington Arcade, an 18th century shopping passage, selling the best in cashmere, jewellery and luxury items, is the Museum of Mankind. The ethnographic collection of the British Museum contains 750,000 objects representing the indigenous populations of North and South America, the Pacific Islands, Australia, Africa, Asia and Europe. Equally fortunate in its setting as its famous parent, the building can also be appreciated in its own right. It was designed by Sir James Pennethorne, who also created the Public Record Office and the Ballroom of Buckingham Palace. Pennethorne was a pupil of John Nash, his adopted son, and this building was completed under Nash's tutelage.

The historic strand between today's use and the building's early purpose as a centre for the University of London's administration can be seen in the statues outside, which include such scientific and philosophical luminaries as Isaac Newton, John Milton, Adam Smith, Galileo, Aristotle and Archimedes. For the best view I stand on the other side of Burlington Gardens. This scholastic gallery of sculpture represents the two disciplines from which ethnographical studies emerged whilst the impressive classical exterior symbolises a place dedicated to learning.

The entrance hall continues in this style, but the exhibition rooms have been altered. However, the Reading Room is still intact and handsomely panelled, and the double height room on the *piano nobile* is finely decorated with a first floor view over Mayfair. The British Museum collection moved here in 1970, and now there are plans to move it back to the British Museum when the British Library opens in 1998.

I was absorbed by some of the artifacts, particularly the embroidery on the Ethiopian textiles, in a display called *Secular and Sacred*, showing tribal importance through the amount and intricacy of embroidery on the clothes. The first time I saw these I wondered how many textile and fashion designers have been inspired by this room, or by the Benin horse quilts. The African art and carvings are of the type which influenced Picasso. On another visit I talked to some textile students from the Central School and St Martin's College of Art, who were doing just what I had supposed; one was as bowled over by the two horse quilts as I was, and had sketched them.

How would, or how could, you try to compete with the colours and textures of this collection? Better not, so the Café Colombia is probably about right; it is cool and calm with blonde wood, although there is a danger that even this style could engulf every restaurant design in the capital and become standard. I make a plea for variety of materials and styles. The glass tables in front of the black bar and director-type chairs covered in linen are stylish, and the frosted glass windows cocoon you from the bustle of Burlington Gardens and the nearby arcade. At least first thing in the morning and late afternoon, this is a sanctuary from the crowds in Piccadilly and Bond Street. The peace is a surprise and the ambience, contrasting with the sensational collections, is fortunately not diminished by the ubiquitous mobile phone user conducting business here. Museums and gardens must be made into 'no go' mobile areas soon, before it's too late!

The prices reflect the area but the café links with the Museum only in name and through some stylish glass cases of merchandise. However, it is in tune with its district, synonymous with luxury. The coffee is excellent but tea is not served because of the coffee company's sponsorship agreement, which overseas visitors may find a little odd. Appropriately fashionable sandwiches made with Eurocentric breads, not ethnographical are filled with Parma ham and Brie; the ultimate indulgence is the chocolate cake. The background noise of the coffee machine, a spread of papers and friendly staff make this museum café one of the few in the metropolis to which I can ascribe the term *'café society'*. The café is more popular with business people than the Museum's visitors. Lunchtime is full with those who labour in Mayfair. And even the

 costermonger who pursues his business selling fruit outside the Museum complements the style; he is dressed in a smart full-length grey frock coat!

Museum of Mankind

6 Burlington Gardens, London W1X 2EX. Tel 0171 323 8043 Fax 0171 323 8013.
Open: Mon-Sat 10-5, Sun 2.30-6.
Closed: Jan 1st and Good Friday, early May BH, Dec 24-26 incl.
No admission charge.
Café: seats 50. Open: Mon-Sat 10-4.30, Sun 2.30-5.30.
Tube: Green Park, Piccadilly Circus.
Buses: 8, 9, 14, 19, 22, 38.

Royal Academy of Arts

Burlington House, Piccadilly, London W1

A rt and food are truly interwoven in the history of the Royal Academy. It gives me pleasure to record that feasts and dinners have been an important element of the Royal Academy since its inception in 1768. Artists' feasts and convivial discussions were held frequently, and always before a new exhibition. In the early days van Dyck invited artists to dine with him at home. Happily the tradition continues; an annual dinner is still given before the opening of every Summer Exhibition.

The Academy is the oldest fine art institution in the country, was formed from groups of artists and for its first hundred years was located at Somerset House. The names on the list of the first members are a roll call of the arts in the late 18th century: among their number are the painters Richard Wilson, Benjamin West and Thomas Gainsborough. Their illustrious 19th century successors were the architect Sir John Soane, J. M. W. Turner, John Constable, and Lord Leighton who later became president. His frescoes at the V&A have just been restored.

From the beginning Academicians had to be practising artists in order to be elected and serve on the governing council under the President. After Somerset House, the Academy moved twice, first to Trafalgar Square, at one end of the National Gallery designed by William Wilkins and finally to the present site off Piccadilly in Lord Burlington's remodelled Palladian house. The work was carried out by Sydney Smirke, whose brother Robert designed the British Museum.

Today as many as 60 students are taught by practising Academicians. In a continuing history of improvements, the latest additions were designed by the architect Sir Norman Foster, an associate Academician. In a new classical space called the Sackler Galleries he has created a gallery for the display of the permanent collections of sculpture. The junction of the new gallery without any interruption, with the older facade, is brilliant; glass treads on the stair and in the floor provide a transparent view, down into what was a former well, of more sculpture on the ground floor. The roof of the original well has become a plinth for displaying the sculpture. A marble relief by Michelangelo of the Virgin and Child with the infant St John, the Academy's most treasured possession, is now mounted upon one wall in a stone frame. The Sackler Galleries have become an integrated element in the main building and are one of the most exciting places for viewing art in London. Look down or up through the skylights to the sculpture and experience a completely different atmosphere from the Victorian galleries.

The Academy followed the training ideal of the French Academies, which were founded in 1648. From 1769 to 1790 Sir Joshua Reynolds gave discourses which established the principles of teaching. His maxims focused the students on the diligence of *'studying the great works of earlier artists'*, and he encouraged them to *'strive for fame by capturing the imagination'*. Sir John Soane, professor of Architecture, was elected as an Academician in 1806 and, from 1809-1837, gave his illustrated and influential discourses on architecture. Exhibitions have been held continuously from 1769. At the Summer Exhibition works are for sale to any who can pay the price. The Academy has always mounted large special exhibitions, now commonly known as *'blockbusters'* which generate queues of would-be viewers the length of the courtyard of Burlington House.

The spectrum is wide ranging and represents many schools. Few people, on the other hand, know that the RA has a considerable permanent collection, accumulated via the system of asking each new Academician to donate a piece of work. This includes work by Reynolds, John Constable, Sir Thomas

Gainsborough, G. F. Watts (whom we shall meet in Surrey), and W. P. Frith, who painted the panoramic scenes of ordinary Londoners at leisure. To set the scene, above the portico entrance from Piccadilly there are celebrations in sculpture of great artists, just as there are of scientists nearby at the Museum of Mankind.

In 1763, the Society of Artists, later incorporated before becoming the Academy, dined as one body for the first time at the Turk's Head tavern. The dinner for 60 cost £9 but extras such as hams and two geese, 45 tankards of porter, lemons and cheese, and 24 papers of tobacco totalled £1710s2d. As the Academy prospered, so the number of guests increased to 100. At one dinner in 1784 whilst the members were given Claret, Port, Madeira and Caravella, the servants had porter and shared a bottle of Lisbon and Port between three of them. One wonders about the efficiency of the service after this libation!

You would expect to find a cultural continuum in such a famous café or the refreshment rooms, as they were called in the 19th century. The panelled room, with terracotta walls similar to the Victorian galleries, is more redolent of the gentlemen's clubs nearby. However, sitting beneath a frieze painted by Leonard Rosoman, one is connected with art and the food does not disappoint. All dishes are beautifully presented and quality is consistently high, in no way inhibiting but inviting. Visitors help themselves, although staff are on hand to guide where needed. The cold selection includes large white bowls of salad which reflect the seasons, with excellent dressings, a hint of cumin in the bean salad and very good bread. Soup might be pumpkin and celeriac, or leek, carrot and broccoli in winter. The idea of being able to have some good cheese, salad and bread at a fair price is well received. Staff serve the hot food; a baked chicken with spring onion sauce is the type of light luncheon that a gallery visit requires, not too heavy but sustaining. The selection is so good that you need to go round again in case you have missed something first time. The puds are worth breaking your diet for! Difficult to choose from lemon tart, rhubarb in season, with apple and ginger, chocolate ganache, and always a fresh fruit compote. This is an attractive place to meet and eat. As the restaurant is always under pressure during a popular exhibition, the best idea is to go with a friend, one to find a table and the other to carry the food!

Royal Academy of Arts

Burlington House, Piccadilly, London W1V 0DS. Tel 0171 439 7438
Fax 0171 434 9837.
Free admission to Galleries, fee for exhibitions.
Open: all year Mon-Sun 10-6 except Good Friday and Dec 24-26 incl.
Last admission 5.30.
Restaurant: seats 140. Open: 10-5.30 every day.
Tube: Green Park, Piccadilly Circus.
Bus: 9, 14, 19, 22, 38.

Sutton House

Homerton High Street, Hackney, London E9

Sutton House is a rarity. It is the oldest family house in existence in East London. The National Trust which acquired it in 1938 have recently brought it alive in partnership with the community. It has become a focus for the neighbourhood with café, a performance base, as well as a superb educational resource for the cohorts of children who visit.

The house was built in 1535, at a time when Hackney was a small country village and city merchants were in the ascendancy. Hackney's situation, some three miles from the unhealthy vapours of the city, presented a more attractive place for merchants and courtiers to build their new homes. Sir Ralph Sadleir was one such courtier and secretary to Henry VIII's chief counsellor Sir Thomas Cromwell, when he built the house at the age of 27. As he progressed he became a landowner, a respected diplomat, and possibly to show off his success he built in brick, a new material. The estate included a substantial garden running down to Hackney Brook. He later sold the house to a wealthy wool merchant in 1550. Did Sadleir, one wonders, know Andrew Boorde, Henry's physician, whom we meet in Sussex? (see page 88.)

Sutton House, however, takes its name from the exceedingly rich Sir Thomas Sutton who bought the tannery next door and founded Charterhouse school and hospital. Succeeding owners embellished the house adding a more important staircase, wall paintings and gilding to the stone fireplaces. And, as with many other Tudor houses, it was given a new façade of sash windows and new roof line to present a more Carolean appearance.

The chequered history includes a mix of uses. One was a school, which was separated in a private wing. It was then bought by a local rector who added the appealing Wenlock Barn in 1904, which gave the house another dimension, in use and style. By this time Hackney had changed and the larger houses split up, therefore the Barn would have provided a much needed community use. It is designed appropriately with Arts and Crafts character, using brick and oak in a style which other philanthropic settlement buildings adopted. Those which opened in the East End at this time were Toynbee Hall, and the Whitechapel Art Gallery designed by Harrison Townsend in 1901.

What I gain from this house is a sense of continuity, the community focus that was sought at the turn of the century. It also holds distinct memories for me as I gave a small reception here one Christmas in one of the exquisite panelled rooms with the hearth ablaze and the table laden with Elizabethan and Jacobean sweetmeats and subtleties.

The little café has been located in a borrowed space, a well placed conservatory that is friendly because of its scale; you order from a tiny bar and the food is brought to the tables. It is quite definitely part of the visit. From a micro-kitchen they manage to make and serve good soup, a fish dish, and such light dishes as stuffed pancakes. Perfectly acceptable fare. It is attracting those who work nearby and providing something you would not find in a high street, namely conviviality. The downside is that it is small and popular; you may have to take another turn around the house, which will not tax anyone.

It would be impossible, without evidence, to record Sir Ralph Sadleir's dinners. But as a rising star with a house he would have entertained. He may have offered his guests such dishes as boiled onions with raisins or a dish of whiting (the café does serve whiting) or a pottage which is a very thick soup of peas and beans. And if he wanted really to impress he may have served some of the latest imports from Portugal, oranges, or Portynggales; these appeared on a banquet for the Skinners' Company in 1560. In the 16th century merchants and noblemen ate well. This was the heydey of English beef, bread and beer and earned England this accolade from Fyne Moryson's itinery, 1617: *'English cookes in comparison with other nations are most commended for roasted meates'*. Being near the Port of London, the house may have had *fysshedays*. These were important in the second half of the 16th century to support sailors and also to save meat. This may sound topical, but fortunately we have not yet reached the point where a Government decrees that we eat fish on certain days! Surprisingly, the *fyssheday* was not Friday but as William Cecil advised in 1563, a Wednesday!

Sutton House

2-4 Homerton High Street, London E9. Tel 0181 986 2264 Fax 0181 533 0556.
Open: early Feb-Nov Wed and Sun and BH (except Good Friday), 11.30-5.30 and Sat April-Oct 2-5.
Admission charge. Free to NT members.
Café: seats 30. Open: all year (except Christmas) Wed- Fri 11-11. Last orders 10.
Sat, Sun and BH Mon 11-5.
Tube: Whitechapel.
Rail: Hackney Central.
Bus: 22B, 30, 236, 253, 276, W15.

Victoria & Albert Museum

Cromwell Road, South Kensington, London SW7

The V&A is the most wonderful museum I know, it really has no equal; large but always welcoming, this is like a visit to an old friend. It must be among everyone's favourite. With its vast courts, collections and corridors there are still intimate spaces and a congenial restaurant which provides peace and good taste. Spending a day here is the best of all possible treats.

The South Kensington Museum (named the Victoria and Albert in 1899) was founded in 1852 after the Great Exhibition and an enquiry into the state of design in England. The enquiry confirmed a concern that England was behind her continental counterparts in industrial design, losing the quality she had achieved in the 18th century. It was the first museum in the world to develop a policy of collecting decorative arts, and the idea of buying from manufacturers was innovative. Most museums were founded on private collections. The Great Exhibition of 1851 itself provided much of the founding collections, in particular the Indian collection.

The V&A building was not built as an impressive Neo-Classical monument, such as the Fitzwilliam Museum in Cambridge, the British Museum in London or the Ashmoleum in Oxford. Some of the first buildings were unprepossessing, shed-like structures which earned the Museum the nickname of *'Brompton Boilers'*. Many of the rooms, however, were designed and decorated as art works in themselves. One stunning gallery, completely furnished by Minton & Co., includes columns and tiles as part of the design. (This is now being restored to its former glory, having been encased in wood!) Later a more impressive entrance was added in Brompton Road which is now the main approach.

Among the rooms or *'courts'*, is the Cast Court, which is filled with massive plaster casts of original sculptures, designed to improve taste and to enable students to copy, from the *'Antique'*.

The fashion, sculpture, ceramics (I particularly liked the late 18th century English collection), woodwork, metalwork and jewellery galleries are marvellous and the collecting policy continues today. There is a complete room furnished by Frank Lloyd Wright. The V&A's strength is its acquisition of whatever is best in the decorative arts and design.

Three rooms formed a suite of refreshment rooms: The Grill Room by Sir Edward Poynter, tiled in white with blue decoration, executed by women; The Morris Room (William Morris was a regular visitor), closet-like with dark green panels; and The Gamble Room, a room in the round, completely tiled, pillars and all. These rooms are now shown as exhibits rather than functional eating rooms. The Grill Room still offered refreshment in 1933. Prince Albert commented on the design of the first restaurant, an innovative development which opened in 1856. Henry Cole reported to the committee that no visitors had to be *'removed for drunkenness'* but there was a *'large consumption of tea and coffee'* as there is now. All appears to have been decorous and the caterer returned a profit of £17 in the first year!

Perhaps I could be described as a V&A groupie; for over 30 years I have lingered and studied in the Museum, frequented the old restaurant, for some time managed the New Restaurant and made a great number of friends. The New Restaurant is now located in the Henry Cole Wing on the lower ground floor. One of its best features is the vaulted, exposed brick and York stone floor area, called *'the street'*, which contrasts with the larger, serviceable space, where the food is presented. The restaurant is part of the Museum. It is near the 19th century refreshment rooms, and there are connections in the design with the collections. Pieces of majolica and tiles are incorporated into the design. Service is principally self help from recently added counters.

The food is good, always made with fresh ingredients and with regard for the seasons; it is a successful formula. Comforting hot dishes such as chicken and celery pie and that cornerstone of English fare, steak and kidney pudding, mix with some continental tastes such as *aubergine Parmigiana* and *'cosmopolitan'* flavours with, among others, Goan dishes. The cold table offers homemade mousses, salmon terrine and excellent salads where each ingredient is discernable, not covered in thick mayonnaise. The soup is fresh and changes every day, and puddings such as hazelnut and coffee cheesecake, have fans, whilst shortbread and cakes

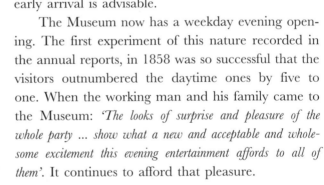

are dependable. The staff devise menus to reflect the major exhibitions. Sunday brunch is popular, so early arrival is advisable.

The Museum now has a weekday evening opening. The first experiment of this nature recorded in the annual reports, in 1858 was so successful that the visitors outnumbered the daytime ones by five to one. When the working man and his family came to the Museum: *'The looks of surprise and pleasure of the whole party ... show what a new and acceptable and wholesome excitement this evening entertainment affords to all of them'*. It continues to afford that pleasure.

Victoria & Albert Museum

South Kensington, London SW7 2RL 6JQ. Tel 0171 938 8500 Fax 0171 938 8379.
Open: Mon 12-5.50 Tues-Sun 10-5.50. Late evening opening Wed 6.30-9.30.
Closed: Jan 1st and Good Friday, early May BH, Dec 24-26 incl.
Suggested donation.
Restaurant: seats 200. Open: 10-5.
Tube: South Kensington.
Bus: C1, 14, 74.

East Sussex

Kent

Surrey

Batemans

East Sussex

There are several reasons to make an excursion to Batemans. Literary historians will be fascinated by connections with Rudyard Kipling who lived and wrote here. Social historians by the mill and village and art historians by the house and contents. Nor will vintage car enthusiasts be disappointed with Kipling's 1926 Rolls Royce; he was a committed motorist and kept diaries of the tours he made in his motors. For Kipling *'the motor was a time-machine'*.

Batemans, a Jacobean house built in 1634 of sandstone, a little later than Crossways (see page 97) was given to The National Trust in 1940. Like Crossways, it lies in the iron-producing area of the Weald, not originally a farmhouse, rather the house of a wealthy iron master. With few alterations and additions, (most it seems by Kipling himself), it remains a fine example of this period. Batemans is essentially Gothic, part of the continuing Elizabethan tradition, with just a hint of the Renaissance in the pilasters at the ground floor entrance of the triple porch (Crossways has a double arch). It is English to the core with brick chimney stacks, pleasing stone mullions, gables and finials. Batemans was a fitting house for the man who said he felt he had come home. *'England has taken me'* he wrote after he and his wife bought Batemans. *'We discovered England, which we had never done before.'* Kipling had lived in London, America, and as a child and young journalist in India.

When Kipling bought the house, he modernised it, pulled one mill down and converted the other to provide his own electricity generator. The furniture and furnishings reflect an Edwardian sensibility for the 17th century, when craftsmen respected and knew their materials. Kipling's contribution is largely the result of his time spent in India — rugs, silver and gifts which all look well in the panelled rooms. There is an accomplished oak staircase and late 17th century walnut parlour. Kipling was an eclectic collector; other decorative arts included a Tiffany lamp, Chinese blue-and-white, Delft and gifts which reinforce the singular aesthetic of this house.

No doubt Kipling's relationship by marriage with Edward Burne-Jones, his wife's uncle, and his own uncle Sir Edward Poynter, who designed the magnificent grill room at the V&A, is pertinent. Kipling's father painted watercolours; there are five in the Elsie Kipling's sitting room. (His painting of a delightful menu card for his 25th birthday portrays Kipling riding on a camel!) Kipling commissioned Ambrose, Sir Edward Poynter's son, to design a double oast house, in true Arts and Crafts tradition, setting the new sympathetically against the old.

The house and garden are also in harmony. Kipling planned the walled garden with borders onto which the tea terrace looks. He wrote *The Glory of the Garden* and *Puck of Pooks' Hill*, where the fabric of Sussex is intertwined with its history, while living at Batemans. The rose garden leads to the less formal gardens with shrubs and bulbs; best in spring. Roses run riot in the summer, especially Maiden's Blush, a 15th century species. From there you can walk along the bank of the River Dudwell to a restored mill which grinds wheat.

Kipling wrote *'Our England is the garden, it abideth not in words'*. The scale, colour and the diversity, formal and less formal, need to be seen. Batemans is a little haven surrounded by the land Kipling bought with it. Inspired by the view of the Weald, this prodigious writer and Nobel Prize winner, wrote looking out from his study, seated at a 10-foot long desk which any writer would covet. Kipling's works are intimately bound up with Sussex. As G. M. Trevelyan wrote *'he fell under the charm of rural Sussex, its folk ... and traditions'*. And he took a special interest in the herb garden. It would be interesting to discover how he entertained his illustrious guests, Rider Haggard, the Burne-Joneses and Stanley Baldwin, his cousin. Did the Kipling household I wonder run to Edwardian excesses or tea parties on the terrace?

The small tea-room is located in one of the outbuildings but takes you straight onto a delightful garden. Sitting there on a summer's morning is bliss, with a fine view of the house. The lay-out and width of the room mean that there is often a queue, but they have taken the trouble to research some local recipes. I tried Sussex black cake, a fruit cake. The lunches served from the counter are suitably vernacular — cottage pie but no Sussex Pond Pudding or Sussex Ale, although Burwash was once in the centre of hop-growing country. Wheat grown on the estate is used in the baking and sold in the shop. This is a rare connection, there are too few places doing this. Perfection would be a less cafeteria-like design in this rural setting.

It is difficult now to imagine as you walk down the village street that just over a hundred years ago this was a town coping with severe poverty and political strife. Today it looks so content and well heeled as though butter wouldn't melt in its mouth. John Coker Egerton who was vicar from 1857-88, tells a different story of illegitimate births, of a pub with a reputation known as the *'rough'* and of villagers *in extremis*, stealing chickens and waiting for their free bowls of soup at Christmas. Egerton also recorded that Harvest Homes were held at Batemans on two successive years, 1857-58 in early October. *'Down to Batemans where there was dinner for about 50... Good beef and pudding ... good appetites brought by ye men.'* The prize for the best allotment holder given at the dinner was 12s. On December 1st 1885, the day before the election, a year when crops were scanty, (when farming folk exercised their right to vote for the first time) Egerton had to keep order at meetings where feelings ran high. His diary entry: *'Bentham Fuller put out a big loaf labelled Gladstone and a little two-penny one labelled I think Salisbury'* illustrates the level of interest and sense of humour. Political views were a theme of life in this village which I imagine Kipling would have liked. For he was a patriot, poet of sense, civilisation and the barrack room, whose songs were sung in music halls, and who got beneath the skin of the country.

Batemans

Burwash, Etchingham, East Sussex TN19 7DS. Tel 01435 882302.
Open: Sat-Wed end March-Oct 11-5.30. Open Good Friday.
Admission charge, free for NT members.
Tea-room: seats 58 and terrace. Open: 11-5.
Rail: Etchingham 3 miles.
Road: A265. Parking 200 yards (wheel chairs at ticket office near car park).

Charleston Farmhouse

East Sussex

Charleston is a vernacular farmhouse of flint and brick that was the home of the artists Vanessa Bell (married to Clive Bell) and Duncan Grant. The setting is idyllic and it is the only place with a complete example of their decorative work, leaving a unique creation accomplished over sixty years. It is a exceptional legacy. Charleston became a real haven for other artists and writers who found their muse here. The *genius loci* remains.

'Bloomsbury' was the name given to a group of friends who first met at Cambridge in the 1890s. After university *'The Apostles'*, intellectuals, continued to meet at Fitzroy and Gordon Squares, where on Thursday evenings *'whisky, buns and cocoa'* kept them going while they talked into the night. Lytton Strachey described the Bells as *'a sprightly couple'* and their first house in Bloomsbury without painted furniture contrasts with Charleston: '*The Drawing Room had no carpet or wall-paper, curtains some blue and some white, a Louis XV bed, two basket chairs, pianola ... early Victorian mahogany table.*'

Roger Fry was also a member of the Bloomsbury Group. His achievement in bringing to England work by Cézanne and the other Post-Impressionists formed the first and second Post-Impressionist exhibitions in 1910 and 1912. These had a powerful influence on the Bells and Grant. It is difficult to imagine just what a sensation these pictures caused. They were also a catalyst for the Omega workshop, a co-operative arts venture making, decorating and selling furniture and ceramics. Not a commercial success, but a forerunner of the many successful crafts galleries around the country. The words *'exuberant'*, *'colourful'* and *'joyous'* describe Vanessa and Duncan's work at Charleston. Vanessa's sister, Virginia and her husband Leonard Woolf discovered the house when they moved to the area, just after the First World War, when Virginia wrote to Vanessa saying *'if you lived there you could make it absolutely divine'*. Although run down, Vanessa and

Grant gradually turned the farmhouse into Bloomsbury in the country. Charleston was cold in the winter, and electricity was not put in until 1933. Vanessa and Duncan, therefore, stayed either at their flats in Bloomsbury or visited the South of France using Charleston as a summer house. Charleston remained the home of Duncan Grant until he died in 1978.

From a state of neglect it was painstakingly restored by The Charleston Trust. What was a private home, decorated for the artists' own pleasure, became an art work. Walls, doors, tables, fireplaces were painted, lampshades, and textiles were designed especially for this house. Several motifs are repeated. In Clive Bell's study a repeated circle and running pattern painted by Vanessa around the fireplace is taken up in the fabric covering a chair. The same design crops up in the wonderful dining room table, also painted by Vanessa. Every surface including the screens, walls, and a trunk by Grant, with Cézanne influence, is painted with a muted English palette: grey, green, yellows. The colours and textures that inspired Vanessa and Duncan on their trips to France have been transported, absorbed and created anew in Sussex. The house developed; they painted and the collections grew. They were given paintings by Picasso, Derain, and Renoir which hang with their own work. Charleston, therefore, is exceptionally rich showing a complete style and its influences all in one location.

Not a tea-room as such but very acceptable refreshments are served in Charleston style — imaginatively. There are no frills or fancies and a functional urn on a trestle table is used to make tea whilst round, plump, rural cakes are presented on sunflower plates and tea is served in green mugs! On one visit I took my generous slice of cake into the walled garden where I sat looking out over the farm buildings and country in the company of the farm cat. This little space is ideal for digesting the visual feast indoors. The gardens are also charming. On study days groups are treated to buffets laid out on a large table with platters of cheese, good bread, grapes, tomatoes and basil, robust and fresh, presented with panache. The staff are delighted to provide a similar repast for any group tour. There is a generous attitude to visitors and their needs, which is not common enough. The shop sells books on the Bloomsbury Group, and specially commissioned decorative arts, ceramics, textiles and Charleston presents small related exhibitions and hosts literary festivals.

To round off the visit you should make the short journey to Berwick Church where you will see murals painted by Duncan Grant, Vanessa Bell and her son Quentin Bell, commissioned by Bishop Bell of Chichester (no relation) in the War. The third leg is Monk's House, six miles away at Rodmell, the home of Virginia and Leonard Woolf and atmospheric in a completely different way. The garden looking across to the Downs was laid out by Leonard Woolf and is still maintained in the same fashion, with the continuing help of the villagers.

Charleston Farmhouse

Nr Firle, Lewes, East Sussex BN 86LL. Tel 01323 811265 Fax 01323 811268.
Open: April-Oct Wed-Sun and BH Mon 2-5. Mid July-early Sept 11.30. Nov-Dec Sat and Sun 2-4. Connoisseur's day Fri.
Admission charge.
Tea-room: 3-5 weekends only. Free access.
Rail: Brighton or Lewes.
Bus: 30 from Brighton,126 from Lewes.
Road: A27.

Pevensey Castle

East Sussex

Rarely is one is able to return to a place one knew as a child and find memories still alive. My parents had taken us out from boarding school in Sussex and I remembered the trip to Pevensey where two ladies served brimming bowls of strawberries in the tea garden, under the trees of a 19th century cottage, the other side of the Castle wall. This closed in the 1960s and I was delighted to find, some five years ago, that it had been restored and re-opened to serve its original purpose.

On my most recent visit I learnt that the two ladies were sisters, the descendants of the Custodian, S. Covell, an entrepreneur after my own heart who advertised locally in 1885 *'that he was now prepared to supply at the New and Commodious Cottage at the Entrance of the Castle Keep, light refreshments of every kind.'* In the late 19th century Pevensey was marketed as a serious excursion and two railway stations were built to accommodate the Victorian visitors.

Pevensey was once a harbour, and a Cinque Port, until 1564. It was also a centre of smuggling. One third of all the gin and tea smuggled into England was landed here. The Castle also has a remarkable history. It has been a fort since Roman occupation, when the first keep was built and the Saxons fought and annihilated the Britons living here in the 5th century. Five hundred years later, the Norman keep was added after William the Conqueror landed making this the base camp. The French knew the topography in advance, through trade, *'wool out, wine in'* and Pevensey was eminently suitable for launching their invasion. Later the Castle was besieged by Simon de Montfort and in the late 18th century Pevensey was a site of the Martello towers, put up as a defence against the French. You can sense the stronghold by walking around the outside walls, and its strategic position from which any occupants would have a entire view over the levels, and up to the Downs. After hundreds of years as a fort, garrison and as a radar post in the Second World War, Sussex sheep are the solitary incumbents. However this terrain of salt marshes produces the finest flavoured lamb — the *pré salé*, much prized in France. The sea cannot be seen any longer, but there is evidence enough of its former importance. In the nearby house, dating from 1076, William also set up the Mint in which Andrew Boorde, physician to Henry VIII and pronouncer on diet and health, lived and entertained. Boorde enjoyed a simple vegetarian diet, and celebrated the importance of garlic, onions and leeks. He emphasised the efficacy of fresh food, but did not favour beer. England had recently started to import large quantities of foreign beer, a fashion which he wrote was *'muoche used in Englande to the detryment of many Englysshe men ...* although, *a naturall drynke for a Dutcheman.'* But he recommended soups,*'stewpottes, and potages'*.

The surrounding country provides good walks up to the Downs and the Pevensey levels are now a Site of Special Scientific Interest, an important habitat for wild life. Water violets and flowering rushes grow here. In Pevensey and in Westham the next village, tile hung houses, early Norman churches and good vernacular architecture abound. A watercolour dated 1852 by Louisa Pine, entitled *'The cottage of people who show the Castle'*, hung in the Towner Gallery at Eastbourne, shows a similarity with those left in the village. Is it too romantic to speculate whether Gilpin and other exponents of the *'picturesque'* visited this ruin?

The Castle and the listed Castle Cottage are now in the care of English Heritage. The Victorian tea-rooms are still surrounded by gardens. The car park in front of the cottage has a somewhat rough surface, but this was the former cattle market and is also listed! The present manager Janet Southouse continues the tradition of hospitality, knows the area well, can answer any number of questions and cooks local food. She even keeps chickens —

at home of course! She has personalised the tea-room, and the food is Super Sussex. Janet cooks and serves all that you would ever expect from a Sussex tea-room: at the weekend, a real roast, beef or local Southdown lamb; Sussex cheese, baskets of scones, meringues, home-cooked ham and old-fashioned crab salads, are on offer; a choice of cakes that stops customers in their tracks, and, the elusive Sussex Pond Pudding! In a recipe for this delicious pudding from Westham dated 1905, suet and currants are made into a dough which is filled with a butter ball (butter and sugar). Blanket pudding is another comforting traditional Sussex dishes which should be boiled in the obligatory muslin cloth.

If you are really fortunate you may meet Janet's Aunt Mollie who is not only able to regale you with Sussex gossip but is a member of the family who still makes Sussex trugs.

Janet sends her young assistants to the local farms to collect the strawberries and other produce for her customers. She truly supports the site and the region, lives locally, once ran a local market garden, and buys everything from the nearby fishmonger, butcher and grocer. Her tea-room is the first drop for a local grower's summer vegetables and salads on his way to Eastbourne. Booking is essential because of the tea-room's reputation.

Pevensey Castle

Pevensey, East Sussex BN25 1LE. Tel 01323 762604.
Open: April-Sept daily 10-6. Winter Wed-Sat 10-4.
Admission charge. Free to EH members.
Tea-room: seats 35 inside, 90 outside. Open: April-Oct 10-6, 7 on Thurs, Fri and Sat Nov-March 10-4. Free access. Tel Castle Cottage 01323 460382.
Rail: Westham.
Road: A27. Parking very near.

Lullingstone Castle

Kent

I must confess that on my first visit I nearly gave up before I had arrived. This may be advantageous; if it is difficult to locate, it may stand a better chance of surviva! The Darenth Valley is a haven where the majority of the natural landscape has been designated as a SSSI. An enlightened council is currently working with other bodies to improve the flow of the river and enhance the wildlife habitat. The valley is sandwiched between arterial roads and a motorway, of which Kent seems to have more than its fair share. Difficult to believe that this tranquil spot is only half an hour from the Old Kent Road in London. Fruit gardens and hop fields are disappearing fast, but you will still find some here and, miraculously, the four villages in this valley are still intact.

The valley shows in miniature an earlier pattern of farming in this, the Garden of England. There is a lovely walk to the castle, following the course of the River Darent. This is well marked and takes you past the Roman Villa and a Norman castle, and under a splendid viaduct. From Eynsford walk or drive across the ford to reach Lullingstone Castle, and the car park, which is located by the Roman Villa.

Lullingstone Castle is a Queen Anne mansion, with an Elizabethan core and a separate, Norman church. The courtyard, now green, was formerly a jousting ground, over which a Tudor keep of 1497 (probably one of the earliest in England) stands guard. The house was built by John Peche, who held an important position in Henry VII's court and entertained the young King Henry VIII here. Originally there were two gatehouses and a moat, but one of the gatehouses was pulled down and the moat filled in when the castle was given a Queen Anne treatment. The Queen visited the house frequently, continuing the association which the family had enjoyed with previous sovereigns.

Walking around the outside of the house, you can see the

Tudor construction in the inner courtyard and great chimney breasts. There are stunning views of the gatehouse, the parkland beyond the church, gardens and lake. The river runs through the estate and a delightful means of approach is from Eynsford station, across the fields or slightly farther, from Shoreham station.

The exterior of the house has a pleasant domestic scale, so the grandeur of the double-height hall is unexpected. An oil painting showing the earlier castle and plan hangs over the 18th century mantelpiece. The 18th century rooms, of pleasing proportions, are panelled and have fine oak floors. I was taken by the glazing bars at the windows, which frame the beautiful view out onto the park. The stately Queen Anne staircase, constructed for her visit, demands to be ascended, and with its very wide treads and low risers, was obviously designed for ladies wearing wide-hemmed skirts.

The bright façade of St Botolph's Church has a stone porch, and services are held regularly. The delicate stained glass windows must be seen, also the ornate plasterwork ceiling which was constructed when the house acquired its new front. The outside elevation shows a line of brickwork inserted above the flintwork, so that the roof could be raised to accommodate the new ceiling.

Doors with linenfold panelling and a spiral staircase take you up to the tea-room in the Tudor gatehouse, one tower of which was restored earlier this century. Two dining rooms look out to the mansion, gardens and cedar trees with unadorned black tables and chairs, and uplighters making a good contrast with the architecture. A wall hanging of a brass rubbing reminds you of the church and the family history.

Sarah Hart Dyke, whose husband's family have owned the house since 1738, is the cook and she prepares food in one of the tower rooms, in a spotless scullery. Lullingstone encourages lingering; allow sufficient time to enjoy this place, bearing in mind that today's Kentish maids have to fetch and carry large trays laden with tea trappings up and down the tower's staircases. The food has a style of its own. There is freshly squeezed apple and carrot juice, and the tea bread (banana and honey) was excellent and thickly sliced; there is also a herb and cheese bread. Good wedges of chocolate, hazelnut fudge, ginger, wholemeal carrot, almond and fruit cake are popular. The scones and sandwiches are welcomed by hungry walkers, whilst those with dogs can order their tea to be brought down under the trees outside the gatehouse. This, as far as I can recollect, is the first gatehouse tea-room I have seen. The owner thoughtfully opens the tea-room until the beginning of the autumn half-term week in October, although the house closes earlier.

It is good to find a connection with William Cobbett. In *Rural Rides* published in 1830, he writes of a breakfast of eggs, milk, gooseberries and currants which he and his son enjoyed at Farningham. Shoreham provides another link with the painter Samuel Palmer, who lived and painted here for seven years. He wrote that this '*cosy*' village was '*full of association that carried you far back into the pastoral life of Merry England years ago*'. Darenth, Lullingstone and the environs, still evoke this idyll.

Lullingstone Castle

Eynsford, Kent DA4 OJA. Tel 01322 862114.
Open: March-Sept Sat, Sun and BH 2-6.
Admission charge.
Tea-room: seats 50. Free access. Same opening times as House.
Rail: Eynsford 0.5 mile.
Bus: 401, limited service.
Road: A225. Parking outside.

Claremont Landscape Garden

Surrey

Claremont is a joy, a living history of landscape gardening. Four of England's most famous landscape architects — Charles Bridgeman, William Kent, Sir John Vanbrugh and *'Capability'* Brown — each brought something new to the gardens, whilst respecting their predecessors' work. It is much smaller than other famous gardens such as Stowe; it takes three-quarters of an hour or so to do the whole turn. However, it is a microcosm of English 18th century taste, having all the correct ingredients. I particularly like the diversity of steep paths, water and views.

Claremont came to the National Trust in 1949. In spite of its proximity to London, it seems like an excursion. I am grateful that over the last seven years my daughter and I and our friends have been able to visit these gardens so frequently.

Claremont's exceptional design history began in 1709 when Sir John Vanbrugh, the architect of Blenheim Palace, built himself a villa at Esher. He sold it to the Duke of Newcastle, who named the estate after his earlier title, Earl of Clare — Clare Mount. The Duke was a committed Francophile in food and patron of the art of cookery. He was relentless in his search for a chef who would prepare *'La Cuisine qui domine en France'*. He was without doubt a gourmet.

The Duke must have approved of Vanbrugh's work for he commissioned him to extend the small house into a mansion more fitting to his position. Charles Bridgeman then developed the gardens, incorporating more of the natural elements, possibly the tree-covered hill. Vanbrugh built the Belvedere — for entertaining and playing hazard — a magical-looking tower at the top of a grassed double bank and a crucial element in the garden's progression. This is open to the public, at weekends only in the summer. As you ascend the hill you reach a high point looking down onto the exceptional grassed amphitheatre. Here, at the top, I pause to observe the whole view — gardens, lake, island and distant grotto. All were constructed between 1715 and 1726. I believe I know every step of each climb and descent, path and circuit of the lake, but I am still surprised by the vistas. In January there are very early camellias; later in February the naturalised bulbs are ablaze under the chestnuts. There is more definition in winter, when it is quite sculptural. Moreover, in winter you are more likely to meet the other hardy annuals, not plants but people who walk here regularly. Later in the summer, when all the trees are in full bloom, the closeness of the traffic on the Old Portsmouth Road is diminished, just a little. The lakeside is perfect for picnics, but crowded on Sundays and the '*Fêtes Champêtres*' celebrated in the 18th Century held here each summer are very popular. Apart from a small period in early January, the gardens and tea-room are open, making it a favourite.

The Duke of Newcastle usually provided King George II with a feast on his birthday November 10th. In 1753, he had recruited a French cook called Hervé, recommended by the Duke of Albemarle, to order a '*Périgueux pye*' (made with truffles) from Paris so that he could provide it on this auspicious occasion. Not to be. Albemarle informed the Duke that '*the pyes*' were not yet in season and never brought to Paris until after the first frost. But by February 1754 the Duke had to let Hervé go, doubting his ability to cook what was fashionable. The soups were too strong, he understood nothing of roasts and his entremets were heavily disguised. Poor Hervé, he was one of several who were sent over to England to take the place of the Duke's most famous chef Cloué (a man who acquired the female nickname Chloë), ordered to leave because of the proclamation against the Papists in 1745.

These culinary connections continue. During the course of the Duke's search for the replacement chefs many letters were sent between London and Paris, and the fame of the Duke's fruit gardens at Claremont spread. Albemarle as a return favour asked if some of the Claremont cherry trees and a few Golden Pippins and Nonpareils could be sent to the Duc de Biron who was planting out his own kitchen garden and had heard from Madame de Pompadour of Claremont's *'great reputation'*.

The plans of the house and gardens in the Belvedere show that these kitchen gardens were large. What other delicacies one wonders must this garden have grown for the table at Newcastle House here and in London? In 1758 Horace Walpole recounts the story that the Duke had ordered the mushroom beds at Claremont to be destroyed after a suspicion of poisoning, writing waspishly: *'and a voice of lamentation was heard at Rameh in Claremont. Chloë* (Cloué, the original chef, had been taken back) *was weeping for her mushrooms and they are not.'*

Back to earth. The little tea-room makes soup; I recall eating mushroom once. The baking is very good but there are not, however, enough connections made in the food or design with Claremont's former glory. This is sad; follics and images in the gardens, or in a vein similar to the small information point, could have provided inspiration for all manner of imaginative buildings for the tea-room and shop. The little weatherboarded tea-room is not an architectural gem and together with the tiny shop, is often overflowing. But a hatch straight onto the gardens, selling ice-cream, keeps impatient children happy and it is just as pleasant to sit outside. We even managed to eat a cream tea on the good, robust, locally made furniture in November.

Many will be pleased to see homemade sausage rolls (good fodder for walkers) and excellent scones which are reliable and reasonable. Seasonal food features; sometimes a cassoulet or hearty stew. The ubiquitous tuna bake has crept in even here. We usually succumb to moist tea-bread or light scones, and carrot cake is popular. Hot puddings are often in evidence. Is it too much to hope that perhaps, just perhaps, a Golden Pippin flan, possibly served with a slice of Cheddar (made in Surrey) or a cherry pie, might crop up some time, in the right season?

Claremont Landscape Garden

Portsmouth Road, Esher, Surrey KT10 0JG. Tel. 01372 469421.
Open: Jan-end March Tues-Sun 10-5 or sunset. April-end Oct Mon-Fri 10-6. Sat-Sun and BH Mon 10-7.
Admission charge. Free for NT members.
Tea-room: seats 43 inside, approx. 26 outside. Open: Jan-end March Sat and Sun 11-4.30. April-end Oct (except Mon) 11-5.30. Nov-mid Dec (except Mon) 11-4.
Rail: Esher.
Bus: 415 Green Line.
Road: A3. Parking at entrance.

Crossways Farm

Surrey

It was certainly not my original intention to lure visitors to those places which rarely open, or gardens which under the admirable National Gardens scheme open for charity one or two days a year. But this single Opening Day, held every two years, is so special that I must include it. Crossways Farm is an architectural pleasure, and also a working farm that takes in guests for bed and breakfast. The Opening is unique because it is a blend of the history and food that I hope to find.

The gentle rolling landscape has been moulded by earlier workings for iron, which give Abinger Hammer and the ponds their name. The River Tillingbourne with its watercress beds (the oldest in the country), where you can buy fresh cress. The tile-hung houses and famous clock at Abinger Hammer set the scene for a visit to the early 17th century yeoman's house.

Crossways Farm, namesake of George Meredith's novel *Diana of the Crossways*, published in 1885, is a splendid example of a Jacobean decorated farmhouse, built to impress in around 1620 by someone who was coming up the social ladder. You enter through a stone arch and are greeted by this friendly house, built in warm materials, sandstone and brick, with handsome chimneys. It is tile-hung on one side, with cut brick for decorative effect on the front elevation. There is an unusual double porch and some delicate arches over the ground floor windows, yet on the side which would not have had to create an impression it is plain. Here you can see the galletting, where mortar is set with small stones to strengthen the construction. This all makes for an absorbing visit and the guidebook is a good purchase.

Once Meredith had found it, when he lived at Box Hill, he used it for several scenes. I do like the *'crackling flames'* of the fire which Diana lights and her apology for the lack of food: *'The best of dinner on bread and butter is that one is ready soon after it, for supper.'*

Inside the principal feature is a grand, for this type of house, yet amusing, staircase, probably the result of the original owner's connections with gentry or his having seen alterations elsewhere at a more distinguished Jacobean house, such as Ham House. This is a perfect example of keeping up with the Joneses — 17th century style. The charm is in the way the risers were placed, as opposed to being built in. The staircase starts well with the classically inspired newel posts and fretwork of the banisters, but the carpenter had trouble trying to make the wide risers fit the space.

I enjoyed my day guiding here on behalf of the Domestic Buildings Research Group of Surrey which assists the owners and the village. The funds raised are given to the local Abinger Hammer school, which was threatened with closure in 1982, saved by community action and is now run as a Trust. Visitors are offered lunch and tea with generosity. Local produce includes Old Scotland Cheddar from Shere, smoked trout and watercress from the Tillingbourne. The enormous choice of cakes, made by the whole village, is set out on trestles under the covered barns. Sometimes 17th century delicacies are offered. Entertainment, in the form of gentle dancing in costume in one of the walled gardens, diverts if there is a queue. Not surprisingly, there are queues but everything is taken in good spirit.

Crossways Farm

Raikes Lane, Abinger Hammer, nr Dorking, Surrey RH5 6PZ. Tel. 01306 730173.
Open: **single day mid-Aug** 11-5.30 every other year. The farmhouse is fragile and the numbers in each group tour are limited. Visitors should telephone 01306 730173 for the next Opening Day.
Rail: Dorking.
Bus: Surrey Hills bus vintage 433 and regular service from Dorking or Guildford.
Road: A25 on Dorking-Guildford approx. 5 miles before Abinger Hammer village left at cross roads, for Sutton and Abinger.

Leith Hill Tower

Surrey

William Cobbett was right when he wrote in 1823, *'They think you mad if you express your wish to avoid turnpike roads'*. This is the best of what I call secret Surrey; off the main roads, full of hearty, booted walkers and rather intense mountain bikers. You can reach this spot, between May and September, in 1950s style char-à-bancs which are run especially for summer excursions.

There are various routes, little used roads, and many way-marked paths; a good Ordnance Survey map and compass are suggested. Several paths lead up to Leith Hill, through the surrounding woodlands conserved by The National Trust who secured the Tower in 1923. The top is the highest point in the region, 1,000 feet above sea level, yet no more than 25 miles from London. On a clear day everyone enjoys spotting landmarks. An engraved orientation plaque directs you to the Downs, Kent and even Crystal Palace. John Aubrey, who lived nearby at Albury, wrote that he could see even see Wiltshire, with a telescope. The tower was built by Richard Hall in 1766, then called the *'prospect house'*, of just two rooms, for his own retirement and the pleasure of others. He considerately provided a little telescope, or prospect glass, for those who walked or rode up to see this remarkable view. Two additions were made, one in 1796 and another in 1864 by the Evelyn family (who own the Wotton Estate) when it was opened to the public.

The diarist John Evelyn lived nearby at Wotton and his legacy are the woods which he helped to plant. His pronouncements on 'salletts' in *Acetaria*, written in 1699, are eloquent. He praised lettuce, as the principal foundation of the universal tribe of *'sallets'*. Garlic, however, was not his favourite, he absolutely forbade *'its entrance into our own salleting'*. That other redoubtable diarist Pepys visited the area staying in Guildford in 1661 at The Lion Inn where he cut some asparagus for himself, describing it as the best he had ever eaten. What an enticing thought — cutting asparagus in a pub garden seems quite inconceivable today! Although those who grow their own or visit to pick-your-own farms will know the joy of cutting and eating this delicious vegetable, which is *nectar* when eaten immediately. At the end of April, asparagus is the vegetable harbinger of summer.

At Leith Hill the bluebells herald spring, followed in May by the rhododendrons. Evelyn introduced Scots firs into this park-like valley which is rich with oak, ash and rowan. The damage that the great storm of 1987 wrought is now being overcome with hundreds of young seedlings. Surrey as Evelyn describes, *'is the country of my birth and my delight'*. Unequivocal Surrey.

The walk up through wooded slopes with their tawny residue of bracken in winter, is a more pleasant climb than the popular Box Hill. From the path starting at Mosses Wood the whole of the Surrey Weald and a glimpse one of the Hammer ponds stretches out south-westwards with few man-made impositions. In summer the walk, although steep, is refreshingly cool depending on your pace; in early spring, invigorating. Old tracks crisscross the area; one is at least 2,000 years old, and another, which crossed the North Downs, was a trade and pilgrimage route from Cornwall to Canterbury. Where the road level has sunk the mossy banks expose the skeletal roots of alder trees. Leith Hill was once, in the 9th century, the site of much bloodshed where, according to Henry of Huntingdon, writing 200 years later *'warriors as thick as corn fought'* a pitched battle with the Danes who had landed on the east coast. They continued their march across the south east from London towards Wessex but were overcome by the Saxons.

Leith Hill is far enough from what Cobbett called the *'Great Wen'* (London) and is surely one of the most beautiful of expeditions. The steep climb does not appear to deter families who consider this area a natural playground. (Who needs theme parks?) When you reach the top there is a cheery welcome from the manager of the tower, a veritable lady bountiful dispensing marvellous slices of cake, tea and information. Together with the breathtaking view, this is the finest reward for your endeavours and nothing more is needed. This enterprising lady sells tickets to the Tower, postcards and a booklet of Surrey tales with her recipes.

The service at Leith Hill is run for The National Trust and a knowledge of the area and commitment to the visitors is noticeable. Homemade cakes are sold from one of the Tower openings; a cup of tea and cake must represent some of the best value in the country. The cakes are good — carrot, banana, Leith Hill fruit cake and a very popular treacle tart. A bowl of filling lentil and onion soup at an amazing price is the real thing.

This sort of food is perfect for walkers and bikers. For a café serving out of what is no more than a cubbyhole, they have devised a remarkable time-and-motion-system, so that gasping, out-of-breath and thirsty visitors wait no more than a few moments. The best news is that all this is open every weekend of the year. The manager's dedication to her customers deserves to be recorded. All the water and victuals have to carried up, whatever the weather, even in the snow!

Leith Hill

Nr Coldharbour, Dorking, Surrey. Tel 01306 711774.
Open: April-end Sept Wed 12-5 every weekend and BH 11-5. Winter 11-3.30.
Admission charge. Free for NT members. No interior seating.
Rail: Dorking or Guildford.
Bus: 433, Sun vintage bus in summer then 2.5 miles.
Tel for times 01737 223000 or 0181 541 9366.
Road: A 29/ B2126.

The Watts Gallery

Surrey

Compton falls into two distinct time and cultural zones. A small village on the edge of the North Downs, it is packed with history and inspiration. Compton is set in civilised park-like country, on the Pilgrims' Way, near the Hog's Back. In the older part of the village there is a small parish church, unrivalled in Surrey, with Saxon spire and surrounded by cedar trees. It contains an extremely rare Norman double chancel, positively Durham Cathedral-like engraved Norman pillars and rare Norman balustrades. On a hill at the entrance to the village there is an extraordinary terracotta Art Nouveau chapel and separate cloister built by the painter G. F. Watts's widow in the early 20th century, as a memorial to her husband. Nearby are The Watts Gallery and the pottery which is the site of the tea-shop. Every surface of the deep red brick Romanesque-style chapel is richly decorated, or rather burnished, with gold, copper and reliefs based on Celtic themes and circle of life symbols. This influence has spread to the cemetery, where many headstones have Celtic and Art Nouveau carving in the same red brick.

It is surprising to find such a rich cultural mosaic in one small village. There is a good hostelry, The Withies Inn which has a pleasant garden, while the former White Hart Inn, probably one of the oldest buildings, is tilehung and has a jetty, (the joist supporting the first floor of an upper room that projects beyond the wall of the lower one in a timber-framed house). The Elizabethan mansion of Loseley is nearby on the road to Godalming. The rural seclusion of this part of Surrey attracted G. F. Watts, the Pre-Raphaelite artist, to join like-minded artists and designers to set up their studios here. The Watts Gallery was designed by Christopher Turnor, in 1905, to house 250 of Watts's own works and his studio collections which include ceramics by William de Morgan. It is built in Arts and Crafts style, reflects Surrey traditions, albeit in concrete, and is surrounded by woodland and a charming garden. Turnor was not a professional architect but was briefly associated with Sir Edwin Lutyens who apparently did not approve of the Gallery. Watts's wonderful portrait of '*Lily Langtry*', '*The Wounded Heron*', '*Paolo and Francesca*' and his sculpture are set out in several galleries with warm wood block floors and the barrel-vaulted galleries are decorated with a similar palette to the Chapel. At first the pictures were hung close together, overlapping, and when the Gallery opened as many as five attendants were needed to control the crowds. This is a gallery you will want to revisit and which today you can enjoy viewing in calm.

The idiosyncratic tea-shop, on the other hand, is frequently full and imparts, in winter, a steamy and warm contrast to the Gallery. It is situated in the corner of a small courtyard where Watts and his followers built a pottery. You can see the wooded garden through the high windows and there are contemporary paintings by local artists on the walls. It has a character of its own. The mixture of painted kitchen chairs, multi-coloured tablecloths and the food make it a one-off. There is always a friendly greeting and the service is relaxed; it is conducive to lingering and we are regular visitors. This is definitely not for anyone in a hurry. The food cannot be faulted. Helpings of double cream and jam, homemade and changing with each season, are ladled out with some of the best scones I have even eaten. Jams have a rich flavour; the mixtures of two and more varieties, blackberry, gooseberry, strawberry and blackcurrant are intensely fruity. All sorts of tea-shop indulgences are on the menu: Welsh rarebit, scrambled free-range eggs, local Farncombe bacon and Meadow Cottage ice-cream from Churt, all supporting Surrey.

The cakes are high rise, higher than any usually seen, and marvellous value. Chocolate, coffee, date and walnut are all equally delicious, and it is always difficult to choose. The helpings are more than ample; and there are as many as 50 herb teas to choose from! This place is organic, it grows like Topsy and they cook good hot dishes such as vegetable pie and a bean casserole which are excellent value and vary daily.

The Loseley manuscripts reveal that baked dishes such as orange tart with a rich crust, possibly similar to maids of honour, were made locally. Guildford produced manchets — light bread or rolls and a royal fruit cake, made for every royal visit. The baking tradition is alive and well in Compton.

The excursion is remarkable, a time warp of the best possible kind. Neither the Gallery or the separate tea-shop are part of today's clingfilm society. The Gallery has no barriers to obscure the view; it is a very personal experience, because of scale. And the tea-shop is not part of the rationed culture, not a sign of foil or wrapping is permitted to come between you and the plentiful, golden, buttery tea.

The Watts Gallery

Down Lane, Compton, Guildford, Surrey GU3 1DQ. Tel 01483 810235.
Open: daily Oct-end March 2-4. Wed and Sat from beg April-Sept 11-1 and 2-6.
No admission charge. Donations appreciated.
Tea-shop: seats 60 inside, 100 outside. Open: daily 10.30-5.30, except week between Christmas and New Year.
Rail: Guildford.
Bus: 290.
Road: A3. Parking outside.

WhiteHall

Surrey

Some parts of Cheam date back as far as 1018, though to reach WhiteHall you have to pass through pure suburb. The most important connection is with Nonsuch, one of Henry VIII's 13 palaces, begun in 1538. Nonsuch was literally the palace that was to have, as its name suggests, no equal. It was many turretted, with golden onion-like domes built in Tudor style but with the intention of outshining Fontainebleau. A contemporary Cheam rector wrote, *'What labour, what workmen, what axes, what crowbars, what artists, what sums of money were needed for so great a task'*. Its last owner was Barbara Villiers, mistress of Charles II who, not being fond of hunting and outdoor pursuits, allowed it to fall into disrepair. The materials were used for other buildings and by the end of the 17th century Nonsuch was no more than a ruin. Not a fragment remains today except a public park.

WhiteHall was built in 1500. It is a timber-framed house, now weatherboarded, with three gable ends and a garden, the most impressive building in a cluster of similar houses. The building is especially interesting because it is jettied on both long sides. This is unusual in Surrey, although examples of this construction have been found in Suffolk, at Alborough and in Oxfordshire. The jetty can be a means of gaining extra space and can be a form of decoration which honours an important facing building. This house may have faced Nonsuch Palace, where both Henry VIII and Elizabeth I held court, and also the Church. The Domestic Buildings Research Group suggest that *'WhiteHall, Cheam, was built as a first floor Court Room ... One which Elizabeth I visited on an important occasion'*.

Elizabeth I may indeed have visited WhiteHall, and perhaps held small meetings there; she visited Nonsuch often in the summer between 1559 and her death in 1602, more frequently in the later years. It was the palace she liked best. Masques, balls, revels and tattoos were held there in 1559, the first summer progress of her reign. Later in 1599, during a feast at which a procession of 40 servants carried *'very large joints of beef, and all kinds of game, pastries and tarts'*, a German visitor observed that she *'ate but what she fancied privily ... she seldom partakes before strangers'*.

WhiteHall was also the home of the illustrious writer and art critic William Gilpin, headmaster of Cheam school, now moved to Berkshire where Prince Charles went to school. Gilpin could also be called the father of the *'picturesque'* movement. The house has an exceedingly picturesque mid-16th century porch, which humorously leans streetwards. The *'little room'* contains a small collection of Gilpin's own work and cartoons by William Combe, depicting him as Dr Syntax, illustrated by Thomas Rowlandson. No more than six visitors at one time are permitted in this space!

WhiteHall has been restored to reveal areas of the fabric and, once inside, it is easy to see where the 17th century additions join the original. On the upper floor the small rooms with wide timbers have an amusing camber. They are simply presented; one attic shows a furnished bedroom, such as a late 19th century schoolmaster may have used. A door in the upper chamber has some 17th century graffiti, *'Remember'*, which may relate to the founder of the school, a monarchist. Permanent displays explain the development of similar houses, and show some pottery recovered from a dig in the garden.

The house hosts seasonal events such as book fairs and presentations of historic food and is very much a focal point for the neighbourhood. This is vital for the tea-room is run by a coterie of volunteers who wait on you and bake the homemade cakes. The space, light, view of the garden, the medieval backdrop and the exposed lathe and plaster are very pleasant. They get my vote for simplicity. This small unpretentious tea-room has a character created by the architecture and ambience of light beech cane chairs and tables, under the influence of a committed team. The spick and span atmosphere encourages. You will be refreshed by the prices of the cakes; I can recommend the old-fashioned date and walnut and fruit loaf. Jams and marmalade are also made by the volunteers and sold as the season permits. The income from their endeavours is ploughed back into the continuing care and presentation of this historic house.

WhiteHall

1 Malden Road, Cheam, Surrey SM3 8QG. Tel 0181 643 1236 Fax 0181 770 4666.
Open: all year weekdays 2-5.30, Sat 10-5.30.
These times may be subject to changes, please ring in advance to confirm.
Admission charge.
Tea-room: seats 20. Open: as above except closed between 1-2 Sat.
Rail: Cheam.
Tube: Morden.
Bus: 151, 213, 408, 627, 726.
Road: A232, A2043.

R.H.S. Wisley

Surrey

W*hat is Wisley like?'* asked a friend who had never been there. In one sentence, not just a show garden, but a practical demonstration or *'encyclopedia'* of many types of gardening. The planting is designed to delight, inspire, enthuse and educate us mere mortal gardeners. Wisley is also an experimental garden, which is constantly evolving and changing. But it provides pleasure for anyone, gardener or not. These gardens, established in 1904, are the demonstration gardens of the Royal Horticultural Society, founded in 1804, which has a reputation for organising famous shows — The celebrated Chelsea Flower Show and the more recent Hampton Court Flower Show.

When the Society was formed by Joseph Banks, the object was *'to collect every information respecting the culture and treatment of all plants and trees, as well culinary as ornamental'.* In 1822 a garden was leased from Chiswick House followed by another in Kensington in 1861. Finally Wisley was purchased to become a new *'experimental'* garden. In 1890 when the Prince of Wales opened the first Hall in Westminster he praised the Society for *'devoting its energies to the provision of a great national want — a central Metropolitan Hall'.*

Each section is planned to grow the best, or ideal, for a specific type of soil or environment. Wisley is a series of living garden rooms, some very large, which lead into different open spaces. Unlike a museum, Wisley is able to present ever-changing 'exhibitions', planting for the seasons. I suspect there is always one plant, tree or flower at its best throughout the year.

I always visit the vegetable gardens. These allotments were the first model gardens to be established and were planted during the War. I like to see where I have gone wrong or where I may have succeeded. There are examples of vegetable planting in tubs, (spinach, celery, and shallots), blanching methods and storing techniques with as many as 50 vegetables and 400 cultivars in this one spot. Other model gardens include the family, town and the scented garden, and one designed for those with physical disabilities. The main borders are stunning in high summer as, of course, are the rose gardens with over 200 cultivars. In spring the flowering cherries on the long lawns are a photographer's dream. There are different levels, throughout the gardens; the view looking down from the rock gardens, divided with paths, is one of the many pictures and Battleston Hill is covered with rhododendrons in May. As many as 144 bird species have been noted, and we were thrilled to spot a woodpecker one sunny day. For bird-watching and plant noting, binoculars, diary and camera are vital.

I come here for wonderful invigorating winter walks, best of all in snow. There are good splashes of snowdrops while later in February there is the Lenten rose or hellebore — shades of white, yellow and pink. The witch hazels and viburnums in winter and on sunny days, the intoxicating smell of late spring wallflowers and summer roses provide perfume. Wisley contains many shady areas near the wild garden and seats are strategically placed so that you can appreciate the vistas.

The original buildings are pleasing, built in Lutyens style and house laboratories, offices and an advisory service. These have a friendly air with brick gables and chimney stacks and look out over a tranquil water garden. Members can ask for advice on planting for any soil type or environment. I have many friends who make this a family visit. I can understand the reason. Wisley is a splendid garden for all age groups.

The shop at Wisley is superb and deserves a special mention. Exceptional care is taken in the selection of the merchandise and the shopping floor is spacious, so that there is adequate room to browse among the books, forage among the food items or choose a card or two. Too tempting. The garden centre is another temptation. I must include the fruit stall, where pickings are on sale depending on the season.

As for refreshment, our favourite moments are when we can sit outside on the silvery oak garden furniture and enjoy the vistas of lawns and trees as we lick good ice-creams or munch rock cakes, and quaff tea. Other items on offer in the self-service café include salads and variations on the *'little pie'* theme. There is also a more formal restaurant, an ice-cream parlour and another snack point in the peregrination. Perhaps as the seasons progress greater links will be made between all the marvellous fruits in their fruition and the varieties of vegetables and salads in their prime, with abundance. I believe the best place to soak up the

atmosphere and really relate to the garden, is this large terrace.

For a truly green excursion from London, take a Green Line coach, from Victoria coach station. It travels through Richmond and past Hampton Court and sets passengers down near the entrance to Wisley.

RHS Garden

Wisley, Woking, Surrey GU33 6QB. Tel 01483 224234 Fax 01483 211750.
Open: daily except Christmas Day. Mon-Sat 10-sunset.
Members only Sun 9-sunset.
Admission charge. Free RHS members.
Café: seats 300 inside, 150 terrace, restaurant 50. Open: 10-5.30.
Rail: West Byfleet.
Bus: 415 1.25 mile. Every two hours from London, hourly from Guildford.
Road: A3. Large car park, disabled parking.

Index of names